The End of Liberal Theology

The End of Liberal Theology

Contemporary Challenges to Evangelical Orthodoxy

Peter Toon

CROSSWAY BOOKS • WHEATON, ILLINOIS
A DIVISION OF GOOD NEWS PUBLISHERS

The End of Liberal Theology

Copyright © 1995 by Peter Toon

Published by Crossway Books
        a division of Good News Publishers
        1300 Crescent Street
        Wheaton, Illinois 60187

Cover design: Joe Ragont

Edited by Jan M. Ortiz and Leonard G. Goss

First printing, 1995

Printed in the United States of America

Library of Congress Cataloging-in-Publication Data
Toon, Peter, 1939-
    The end of liberal theology : contemporary challenges to evangelical orthodoxy / Peter Toon.
      p.   cm.
    Includes bibliographical references and index.
    1. Liberalism (Religion)—Controversial literature. 2. Theology, Doctrinal—History—20th Century. 3. Evangelicalism. I. Title.
BR1617.T66 1995   230'.046—dc20   94-45233
ISBN 0-89107-833-9

03		02		01		00		99		98		97		96		95
15	14	13	12	11	10	9	8	7	6	5	4	3	2	1	

To dean and president, Ray Sutton,
the faculty,
the staff,
and the students
of Philadelphia Theological Seminary

Contents

Preface

In this book I attempt the difficult task of introducing non-specialist and (primarily) evangelical readers to modern forms of Christian doctrine and theology, both Protestant and Catholic. The emphasis is on the word *modern*, for I describe both that which did not exist before the modern period and that which partakes of the spirit and ethos of modernity.

But when did modernity begin, and what is modern? In this book I assume that what is generally understood as modern has its origins in the scientific, industrial, and technological revolutions that began in the late eighteenth century and were in full swing at the end of the nineteenth century. However, my primary concern is to describe the varieties of theology that have appeared since World War I (1914-18) and, more particularly, since the 1960s.

Although such expressions as *postmodern* and *postcritical* are used today to point to the latest phase of Western civilization, I have not made use of these phrases except when I am quoting from the writings of others. My reason is that they are imprecise terms and seem not to have any fixed or agreed meaning.

However, I cannot escape using the word *modernity*. By *modernity* I understand the spirit and structures of the modern world produced by capitalism, technology, and telecommunications. This reality is of course global, encircling the earth. Also it is intrusive, entering the soul of each person. Sociologists refer to the effects of modernization as placing an "iron cage" around human life and/or of smashing traditional institutions and moralities as with a "gigantic steel hammer."

The method that I have adopted to describe and analyze modern theology is, I hope, neither too complicated nor too simplistic. I begin by taking a specific tradition of doctrine and theology—that of the Anglican way. I do this case study in order to show the basic differences between doctrine in its pre-modern expression (in this case from the sixteenth and seventeenth centuries) and in its modern expression in and after the 1960s. This comparison introduces the reader to what he should expect in the descriptions of modern theology that are to follow. It also raises appropriate questions and problems concerning recent theology.

Since my reader will now have a general idea as to the ethos and content of modern theology, I proceed to trace its heredity and pedigree in chapter two. Portraying liberal theology as a family with a late-eighteenth-century parentage, I describe the history of the family up to the present time, referring to specific theologies since the 1960s as the grandchildren of the first parents.

When today we think of heredity, we also think of environment. So in chapter three I attempt to sketch the intellectual, social, and cultural environment in which modern theology has developed and been expressed. I do this in broad terms for the whole modern period and in a more detailed manner for the last thirty or forty years. In doing this I suggest that evangelical modes of theology have been affected by cultural context just as much as have liberal forms of theology.

The heredity and environment of modern theology are also concerns in chapter four, where I seek to describe the way theology was affected by and expressed within the 1960s. I do this because I believe that the decade of the sixties was extremely important for both American culture in general and Christian theology in particular.

In chapter five I attempt, with the use of typology, to offer various ways of analyzing post-1960s theology. If I were to take every form of contemporary theology and to examine the system of each theologian, the result would be extremely long, tedious, and repetitive. The use of typology (as developed by social scientists) enables the reader to see the limited variety of intellectual constructs around which the greater variety of modern theologies are built.

Having offered several typologies of modern theology, I choose one of these in chapter six in order by it to analyze recent theological approaches, methods, and systems. The typology I use contains four basic approaches—the deductive, the inductive, the reductive, and the regulative.

Finally, in the epilogue I attempt to look briefly at modern evangelicalism with its varied theologies.

At the end of each chapter there is a list of books under the heading "For Further Reading." This is to guide the reader if he wishes to study further the themes handled in the chapter. In addition, four chapters have appendixes in which I specifically treat Roman Catholic theology. In the ecumenical climate of today there is no satisfactory way of treating Protestant and Roman Catholic theology in isolation from each other.

I have deliberately written in a traditional style, not using inclusive language either for human beings or for God. This represents not a "statement" by me, but a carefully thought-out theological understanding of the use of language to reflect what I call "divine order in creation and in redemption." My commitment is wholly to the equality and dignity of men and women and simultaneously also wholly to the principles of divine order as revealed by God within sacred Scripture. Therefore, I use what is not only the traditional style but also the style that contains within it that principle of divine order. Of course, when I describe the views of others and quote their words I work with their concepts and language.

I dedicate this book to the dean and president, Ray Sutton, the faculty, the staff, and the students of the Philadelphia Theological Seminary in appreciation of their kindness to me during the year 1993-94, when I was a visiting professor at their new campus at 7372 Henry Avenue, Philadelphia.

Easter 1994
Peter Toon

Prologue

This book is intended to be a guide to the variety of forms of contemporary theology. It is also a map of the relationship of modern theologies to each other and to their predecessors. Further, it is hopefully a yardstick by which to begin to make critical judgments and evaluations of the doctrines and theologies offered in the 1990s in both the old-line and the new-line denominations, as well as among both liberals and conservatives.

ON THEOLOGY AND DOCTRINE

A good question to ask right at the beginning of this study is: What is the difference, if any, in meaning between *theology* and *doctrine*? Let us try to get some clarity by beginning with their Greek and Latin roots. *Theology* is from two Greek words, *theos* meaning "God" and *logos* meaning "rational study." From the twelfth to the seventeenth century we find that Roman Catholics and Protestants both agree that theology is the study or science that treats God, His nature and attributes, and His relations with angels, man, and the universe. In brief, it is the science of things divine. Put another way, what was called in Latin textbooks *theologia* is the knowledge of God and what God reveals, pursued not merely for academic ends but so that man should enjoy and glorify God forever. Normally it was studied after preliminary work in the liberal arts known as the "*trivium*" and "*quadrivium.*"

Therefore, *theology* has traditionally been the word that covered and included that whole body of knowledge that (since the nineteenth century) has been subdivided into what we call disciplines (or autonomous subject areas) and that we know, for example, as the study of the Old Testament, the New Testament, the creeds, Christian morality, and the history of the church. In fact, what was once the purpose of the whole science of *theologia*—a systematic presentation of truth as revealed by God and understood by man—has now become one part or discipline of the whole and goes by the title of "systematic theology." As such it is equal to the other disciplines even though it seeks to utilize some of their conclusions in its own presentations.

The profound change in the Western appreciation of what is theology, how it is studied, and for what purpose it is pursued came about primarily because of the adoption of the principles of the Enlightenment within the universities of Europe, particularly in Germany, in the late eighteenth and early nineteenth centuries. (The Enlightenment, it may be recalled, was a cultural movement of the eighteenth century that challenged traditional modes of thought based on authority and in their places set forth critical, rational, and historical ways of understanding.) Theology, along with other subjects in the universities, came under the general principles of "proper evidence" (in contrast to the previous authoritative norms and principles deduced from Scripture and tradition), and as such it was subject to pluralization and specialization.

Here we may stop in our tracks and recall that the word *divinity*, from the Latin *divinitas* meaning either "the Godhead" or "the study or science of God," has also been (and still is) used as a synonym for *theology* in its older and fuller sense. A long time ago I received from the University of London in England the Bachelor of Divinity degree, and my work for that degree included the study of the whole Bible, the creeds, church history, and so on. Today many people in North America gain the degree of Master of Divinity (which used to be called the Bachelor of Divinity).

Over the last century there has been a growing specialization in the disciplines of the post-Enlightenment universities. Academics have become experts in less-and-less knowledge. So we find that within what used to be called the faculty of theology (and is often now called "religious studies") there are subsidiary departments of Old Testament, New Testament, church history, and so on. Among these will be the Department of Systematic Theology. While there is a certain necessary cooperation between these departments, it is often the case that members of each discipline feel a closer bonding with members of similar departments in related institutions of higher learning than they do with members of the next department along the corridor from them. Then there are, of course, professional associations for each of these subsidiary areas, and so each separate discipline has a certain autonomy. And what is true of the university is also true of the seminaries, for they have followed the universities in the way theology is studied.

Students working for their Master of Divinity degree today get a little of many things, but rarely do they receive an ordered, rational understanding of God, His nature, and His attributes from their years within the faculty of theology. Most likely they receive an intellectual, religious box containing an assortment of virtually independent parcels of knowledge that will not easily be tied together. To use concepts associated with Isaac Newton and the law of gravity, we may claim that instead of modern study being centripetal (tending toward one center), it is more often than not centrifugal (flying off from the center). This is well illustrated by the book *What Theologians Do* (Healey, 1970). Its twelve contributors (and each one is called a theologian) provide a description of a specific discipline within the modern faculty of theology. So there are essays in the book by the distinguished academics on these topics—the New

Testament, the Old Testament, the inter-testamental literature, church history, creeds and confessions of faith, Christian doctrine (systematic theology), scientific study of religion, philosophical theology, applied (pastoral) theology, worship (liturgy), Christian ethics, and ecumenics (ecumenical theology). Yet, apart from a brief introduction by Healey, there is nothing concerning the unity of theology as theology, divinity as divinity. Theology is merely described as including these subject areas, and it is pointed out that it is necessary to study all the subjects in order to grasp what is involved in professing Christian belief today. In fact the book could be said to illustrate (from a seventeenth-century and pre-Enlightenment perspective) the rebellion of the disciplines of theology against the classical meaning and purpose of theology as a unitive study.

Theology as the science of things divine is apparently now a shattered spectrum in the West. At best, systematic theology, or as the English Anglicans say, Christian doctrine, is the attempt of one discipline within the Department of Theology to appear to do what the whole science was intended to achieve in earlier times. Regrettably, it is often the case that where it exists, that which is now called systematic theology is something very different from the old subject of theology as *theologia*!

Further, and this somewhat complicates the picture I have drawn, we need to recognize that, especially since the 1960s, theology has also been used to mean the ordered religious thoughts of specific interest groups within, or on the fringes of, liberal denominations. So a person working in any of the disciplines of a faculty of theology or religious studies who supplies an intellectual presentation of a contemporary social concern will both call and find others calling his contribution "theology." Well-known examples are black theology, feminist theology, and liberation theology. What usually occurs here is that a legitimate social concern is set in a religious context, given a justification on religious grounds, made into a call for action, and then called theology. Such a theology will use, according to the stance of the writer, a variety of sources. These will normally include the Christian Bible but may include the holy texts of other religions as well, together with whatever other sources are deemed appropriate and useful in the enterprise. Obviously, the main themes here are not "God, His nature and attributes" understood in the traditional sense; rather they are specific social, political, and economic concerns.

Roman Catholic seminaries often refer to theology under three or four headings—fundamental theology, systematic theology, practical theology, and spiritual theology. In these areas they cover much the same type of material (but from a different perspective) as do Protestants in apologetics, systematic theology, pastoral (or practical) theology, and spirituality. Like Protestants, Catholics have been deeply affected by the winds of modernity—primarily since the Second Vatican Council in the 1960s and thus much later than liberal Protestantism.

It is perhaps obvious to my reader that I much prefer to use the word *theology* in its older, comprehensive sense as *theologia* and to see students getting a comprehensive, unified body of knowledge; but I must be realistic and pragmatic and recognize its contemporary usage. Let us then be clear as to what this modern usage is. First of all, *theology* remains as a kind of umbrella word referring to the title of the faculty wherein the various disciplines of the study of religion are pursued. On the same reasoning it refers to all that is studied in a seminary and is part of the requirements for the Master of Divinity degree. Second, theology refers to the specific work and products of those who seek to engage in the specific discipline of systematic theology. Amongst this small group there will be found a great variety of methods of doing theology and of the use of sources that are deemed to be authoritative. Then also, the different schools of thought within modern theology will be represented (e.g., process and narrative theology). In addition, there will be those attached to the theology of specific writers—the theology of Karl Barth or the theology of Paul Tillich, for example. Finally, *theology* refers to the contribution of specific interest groups and their spokespersons—groups such as blacks, feminists, the poor, and those concerned with the physical environment (the ecologists). In this book we are concerned primarily with the second and third meanings.

Now to the word *doctrine*, which comes from the Latin word *doctrina*, meaning "teaching." It has no specific religious meaning, and so in the past we find that a body of Christian teaching is called *sacra doctrina*, "sacred doctrine." It is sacred or holy because of its subject matter, the holy God. In England I taught for some years that which the Church of England (the Anglican Church) then officially called Christian doctrine, and thus I was known in my college as the tutor in doctrine. (Had I been in Presbyterian Scotland, I would have taught systematic theology.) In teaching doctrine, it was assumed that, as a minimum, I was explaining in a modern way, relevant to our times, the official teaching of the Church of England. Perhaps it is true to say that in general the word *doctrine* is used today primarily of official statements of faith, be they from a denomination, a parachurch organization, a missionary society, or a college or seminary. There is, of course, no reason why it cannot be used of both that which is taught by a specific person, normally a distinguished teacher, and that which is the general position of an interest group. Thus, it makes perfect sense to speak both of the doctrine of John Calvin and the doctrine of the movement for the ordination of women.

ADDRESSED TO THE MIND

This book as a guide, map, and yardstick is primarily intended for the intelligent person who desires to understand what has happened to theology in the churches, seminaries, universities, and colleges during this century, and specifically since the 1960s. I assume only that my reader is intelligent and is able to separate his heart from his mind in the making of judgments. Our task is obviously not to get in touch with our feelings but to exercise our intellects in a major effort of understanding. Theology, whether it be good or bad, is addressed in the first place to the understanding and so must be evaluated intellectually. It is so easy to allow deep feelings of prejudice to prevent even the beginnings of the understanding of those theologies that have names such as black theology or feminist theology or political theology. Also it is so easy, living in what has been called, with good reason, a therapeutic society, to allow not only one's first but also one's last evaluation of a system of thought to be via one's emotions in terms of how it appeals to me or how it meets my needs.

The dominant dualism of today is not between body and spirit but rather between feeling and thought, or emotions and reason. Therefore, it is no doubt appropriate and proper, after the intellectual study of good theology, for the enlightened mind to drop into the heart so that the affections, emotions, and will are rightly informed, motivated, and guided in the will of God by right teaching. However, our task here is both a preliminary and an intellectual one, and it is intended only to inform the mind. It is open to any person of average intelligence who is willing to make the effort to try to comprehend the intellectual streams that have gone into the producing of the nature and content of the modern expressions of liberal theology.

This said, I could begin by immediately launching into a description of representative forms and expressions of modern theology (e.g., liberation theology and political theology), inviting my reader to make a tremendous effort to understand them. Yet this would be like putting someone in front of a computer screen and asking him or her to operate a system for which no previous training had been given. We all know that there is a greater likelihood that a person who has had an introductory training session will be able to operate such a system than one who has not had this benefit.

Therefore, I invite my reader to engage with me in two preliminary intellectual exercises before actually joining me in the description and evaluation of contemporary theologies. First of all, there is the task of establishing the heredity of modern theologies and of ascertaining their pedigree. We need to know whose chromosomes they have and what they have inherited from their forebears. Secondly, there is the task of noting the environment in which these theologies have been born and nurtured, and have come to maturity. Through the work done by sociologists over the last century we are all aware of the importance of the influence of the environment on the way we grow and mature from childhood into adulthood. Likewise, the family of liberal theology has been deeply affected by the European and then the worldwide cultural and political context.

Only when we have some general idea of the heredity and environment of the cluster of theologies that make up what we call contemporary theology shall we really be able to appreciate and judge what it is that they are really trying to say to the churches and to the modern world.

However, before beginning these preliminary studies (which will be the content of chapters two and three), we need to get what I call—for want of a better expression—a bird's-eye view of Protestant theology in the sixteenth and the twentieth centuries. Such a view is necessary because the family tree of the theology of the post-1960s cannot be traced in any simple, direct way to the original doctrines and theology of the major Protestant Churches—Lutheran, Calvinist, Reformed (Presbyterian), and Anglican—of the sixteenth century. As we shall see later, there is a fundamental break in these traditions that began to make its appearance in the early nineteenth century and that has greatly widened in the late twentieth century. So today certain forms of contemporary Protestant theology show few if any signs of belonging to the classical Protestant traditions. This is especially true if we recall what was the original (and correct) meaning of the word *Protestant*, as used at the Diet of Speyer in 1529. A Protestant is he who protests on behalf of the Bible as it was received and interpreted in the early church (i.e., up to A.D. 500).

The best way to provide this view for my reader is, I believe, to take a case study of one of the major traditions of Protestantism. This means choosing from the Lutheran, Reformed (Calvinist), or Anglican traditions. (For my Baptist readers, may I explain that I see the Anabaptist tradition of the sixteenth century as a minor, not a major, Reformation tradition.)

Since I am an Anglican, and since I know this tradition from the inside both as a clergyman and scholar, it seems best to attempt to provide an interesting and brief account of the changing face of Anglican doctrine and theology. This will reveal, I hope, that the contemporary forms of Anglican doctrine and theology, which inform the modern developments in worship and ethics, for example, owe little to the original Anglican doctrine and theology of the sixteenth and seventeenth centuries.

FOR FURTHER READING

Farley, Edward. *Theologia: The Fragmentation and Unity of Theological Education*. Philadelphia: Fortress, 1983.

Healey, F. G., ed. *What Theologians Do*. Grand Rapids, Mich.: Eerdmans, 1970.

Kelsey, David. *To Understand God Truly: What's Theological About a Theological School?* Louisville, Ken.: John Knox/Westminster Press, 1962.

Chapter 1

A Case Study:
The Anglican Way

I n the mid-sixteenth century the Church of England lost most, if not all, of its medieval doctrines, associations, and ceremonies and sought to become a reformed, catholic church, faithful to the Word of God. What had happened to the church on the continent of Europe in Germany and Switzerland had made its impact. The teaching of both Martin Luther and John Calvin (not to mention others such as Martin Bucer and Philip Melanchthon) was received into England and flavored the way the reformation of the national, established church proceeded under Henry VIII, his son, Edward VII, and his daughter Elizabeth I.

THE ANGLICAN WAY—AS IT WAS

The theological basis of the English Reformation is most conveniently explained in terms of its commitment to one Bible, two testaments, three creeds, four councils, and five centuries. This was the simple yet profound approach taken by the most prominent early apologists of the reformed Church of England—John Jewel, Richard Hooker, and Lancelot Andrewes—and shows that they had the same basic understanding of the meaning of *Protestant* as that set forth in Germany at the Diet of Speyer in 1529.

One Bible

For most Protestants today there is no difference between two equations: the first is: one Bible = two Testaments; and the second is: two Testaments = one Bible. Logically there is perhaps no difference; yet for the Reformers, following the patristic and medieval church, the first equation is the right one. To begin with the concept of the unity of the Bible affects the way we approach and view the contents of the whole Bible.

To speak of one Bible is to speak of one and the same God to whom both testaments witness. The Lord God whom Moses met at the burning bush and who inspired the prophets of Israel to proclaim the word of the Lord is the same living God manifested in the life and ministry of Jesus of Nazareth. To speak of one Bible is also to speak both of one self-revelation by this Lord God and the one salvation that He provides. Of course, there is a historical development in the way the revealing and saving God is known and encountered in space and time, but the essential point is that the unity of the revelation and salvation (based in the very unity of God Himself) underlies the differences in historical manifestation.

The Reformers of the sixteenth century insisted on the authority of the whole Bible in the church. Article 6 of the Church of England reads:

> Holy Scripture containeth all things necessary to salvation: so that whatsoever is not read therein, nor may be proved thereby, is not to be required of any man, that it should be believed as an article of the Faith, or be thought requisite or necessary to salvation. In the name of holy Scripture we do understand those Canonical Books of the Old and New Testament, of whose authority was never any doubt in the Church.

In the official *Book of Homilies* there is a powerful sermon on the same theme entitled: "On the Reverend Estimation of God's Word." Further, the prayerful approach to the whole Bible is well caught by the Collect for the Second Sunday in Advent:

> Blessed Lord, who has caused all holy Scriptures to be writ-
> ten for our learning; Grant that we may in such wise hear
> them, read, mark, learn, and inwardly digest them, that by
> patience and comfort of thy holy Word, we may embrace and
> ever hold fast the blessed hope of everlasting life, which thou
> hast given us in our Saviour Jesus Christ.

Of course, the Reformers did not believe that all the books of
the Bible are strictly equal in terms of their value for the church.
Naturally they gave pride of place to the books of the New
Testament (and to the Gospels in particular) in terms of the daily
readings in the lectionary for the whole year.

Two Testaments

The Bible of the early church was what we now call the Old
Testament, and to this was added over a period of time those
writings that we now call the New Testament. In other words,
the one canon was expanded to include the writings of the apostles and evangelists. The new collection certainly had two parts,
but it was one collection. So it was said of it that the essential
message of the New Testament is concealed in the Old
Testament, and thus the basic purpose and forward movement
of the Old Testament is revealed or made clear by the New
Testament. Thus, a key way to read and interpret the Old
Testament is via the use of typology. In the Old Testament are
the types, and in the New Testament are the antitypes; Jesus as
the Lamb of God is the antitype, and the lambs of the sacrificial
offerings of the temple are the type.

Article 7 says this of the Old Testament:

> The Old Testament is not contrary to the New: for both in the
> Old and New Testament everlasting life is offered to Mankind
> by Christ, who is the only Mediator between God and Man,
> being both God and Man. Wherefore they are not to be
> heard, which feign that the old Fathers did look only for tran-
> sitory promises. Although the Law given from God by
> Moses, as touching Ceremonies and Rites, do not bind
> Christian men, nor the civil precepts thereof ought of neces-
> sity to be received in any commonwealth; yet notwithstand-

> ing, no Christian man whatsoever is free from obedience of
> the Commandments which are called moral.

Here the "old Fathers" are the patriarchs of the Old Testament to whom, it is stated, God gave promises unto everlasting life. Further, the moral content of the revelation from God (in contrast to that revelation that was solely for Israel as a theocratic nation with a limited life span) in the Old Testament is seen as binding for all time. As a result, Christians have traditionally been taught the Ten Commandments, which are inscribed on the walls of many Anglican churches. Additionally (and the article does not say this), from the "Ceremonies and Rites" have been taken types pointing to Jesus Christ and the new covenant and inaugurated by His precious blood.

In contrast today, because of the specialization and the division of theology into disciplines in the university and seminary, there is professional study of the Old and the New Testaments. However, there is rarely any study in the modern theological curriculum that presumes and sets forth the unity of the Holy Scriptures and interprets the Old by means of typology. This is nearly as true of evangelical as of liberal seminaries. The logic and practice everywhere followed seems to be that of two Testaments = one Bible, with little emphasis on the unity.

Three Creeds

The Bible as Holy Scripture never existed apart from the church of God in space and time. So it is appropriate to speak of the Bible as an authoritative collection (made by the early church) of authoritative books (the author of each being inspired by the Holy Spirit). The church that made the collection of books had a doctrinal basis. This is found in its clearest form in its creeds, which are summaries of basic biblical themes and teaching. These were used for baptism and for stating what is believed, taught, and confessed by the church.

The creed known as the Apostles' Creed was used as the basis for the confession of faith in holy baptism. Thus, it is simple and is easily committed to memory. That known as the Nicene

Creed was produced by the bishops of the church at the Council of Nicea in A.D. 325 and then fine-tuned at the next council in Constantinople in 381. The Nicene Creed began (in 325) as a statement of what the church holds to be the truth concerning the relation of Jesus Christ to the Father and then developed (in 381) into a statement of God as the Holy Trinity. It became the profession of faith said by all believers in the Eucharist of the Sunday worship of the churches.

The third creed was only used in the West from the fifth century on and is known either as the Athanasian Creed or as the *Quicunque Vult* (the first words in the original Latin). This is longer than the other two and gives a precise statement of the doctrines of the Holy Trinity and of the person of Jesus Christ. In the Church of England it was appointed to be used on Trinity Sunday and on other specific days.

It can be argued that most of the seminal writings of the Reformers, including their catechisms and confessions, were in one way or another expositions of the creeds. This is, of course, also the case with John Calvin's famous book, *The Institutes of the Christian Religion.*

Four Councils

A basic claim of the Reformers was that they wanted to reclaim and recover the faith of the early, undivided church of the first five centuries or so—before the division between East and West and before the beginning of the so-called Dark Ages. So, they laid great emphasis on the teaching officially sent forth from the first four councils—Nicea (325), Constantinople (381), Ephesus (431), and Chalcedon (451). From these councils they learned the fundamental doctrines that answered the questions: Who is God? Who is Jesus? What is the Gospel? However, as the Reformers insisted, they only received these doctrines because it was obvious to them that they were truly faithful to the teaching of Holy Scripture. Further, they fully recognized that such councils could err, and in fact later medieval councils did err.

It is sometimes asked why they did not opt for seven councils, for there were (by common agreement today) seven truly ecumenical councils in which East and West were involved. The answer is that they knew little or nothing about the seventh (Nicea II, 787) and judged the other two (Constantinople II, 553; Constantinople III, 680-81) only to have fine-tuned the Christology set forth in the Definition of the Faith by the Council of Chalcedon in 451.

Five Centuries

This affirmation goes with that of the four councils. It was a recognition that the Reformed Church of England would follow the general lines of development of theology, liturgy, and polity of these five centuries. This included: the recognition of Sunday as the Lord's Day and as the day of worship; the use of the church year from Advent through Christmas and Easter to Trinity season; the reading of the Bible through a structured lectionary; liturgical worship rather than extempore worship; the celebration of the Holy Communion on Sundays and holy days with daily prayer in the morning and evening of every day in the church; and the retention of the three-fold ministry of bishop, presbyter, and deacon.

The doctrine within and arising from this basis and method became both the *lex credendi*, "the law of believing," and the *lex orandi*, "the law of praying," of the Church of England. This doctrine is found within the *Book of Common Prayer* (first edition in 1549; revised editions 1552, 1559, 1662), which provided the services for the public worship on weekdays and the Lord's Day, as well as the occasional offices (e.g., baptism, marriage, and the burial of the dead) of the church.

Hence, the doctrine set forth in the three creeds and articles of religion addressed both the invisible and the visible structure of the form of words of the daily offices, of the administration of the Lord's Supper, and of all the other services. Further, an integral part of the *Book of Common Prayer* is the catechism, which is an exposition of the creed, the Ten Commandments, and the Lord's Prayer. Then, of course, a lectionary is part of this whole liturgy; and where this is followed, the whole Bible is read through systematically each year and the Psalter is prayed once a month.

It has been claimed that the Church of England (and, therefore, the Anglican Communion of Churches developing from it) is not a confessional church like the Reformed and Lutheran (who have their carefully constructed confessions of faith). Even if this claim were true, it is also true to say that classical Anglicanism, Lutheranism, and Calvinism share a common view of what is theology. Theology is reflection on Scripture in the light of the doctrinal position or confession of faith of the church in order to cultivate a right mind that delights to worship God and practice the Christian virtues. This makes theology and doctrine closely and perhaps inextricably linked. Within Anglicanism, the work of theologians may be seen over the centuries not only in careful expositions of the creeds and the articles of religion but also in the traditional *Book of Common Prayer*. The latter has been the basis for reflection because it contains the *lex credendi* in the form of the *lex orandi* of the church.

Obviously, the exposition and teaching of this faith was not identical in all the parishes of England, and neither was it uniform in books explaining the Anglican Way. The Church of England has always had a spectrum of interpretation of doctrine that goes from very Protestant to very Catholic. It has always contained schools of thought or churchmanship ranging from high to low in terms of the use of ceremony and the frequency and interpretation of the sacrament of Holy Communion. What can be clearly said of all theologies genuinely arising from the doctrines of the *Book of Common Prayer* and the articles of religion is that they are classically catholic and Trinitarian in their teaching concerning the Father, the Son, and the Holy Spirit; and they are classically Protestant (or Augustinian) in their teaching that salvation is by the grace of God through faith.

It may be claimed that as long as the traditional prayer book was the basis for worship, it was always obvious to the alert worshiper whether or not the parish priest in his teaching and preaching was straying into other views of God, of Christ, of salvation, and of sin than are provided within the book. Having said all this, I must freely admit that sound, orthodox doctrine, as is found in the successive editions of the *Book of Common Prayer*, lives best in lively, God-fearing hearts and in the devout worship of faithful congregations. No prayer book, however good and however prominent in the pews, can by and of itself preserve godliness and orthodoxy.

THE ANGLICAN WAY—
IN THE PROCESS OF CHANGING

Since the 1960s the churches of the Anglican Way, from Australia to Canada and from England to South Africa, have seen the development and adoption of new prayer books. In some cases they have replaced the classic *Book of Common Prayer* (as in the USA in the Episcopal Church), and in other cases they have come alongside as an alternative to the classic book (as in Canada and England). The actual doctrinal content of these new prayer books, when carefully examined, represents a major revision of that found in the traditional prayer book. This revision is not always immediately obvious because the traditional language of Zion is still used and, further, most worshipers who were brought up in the use of the old book tend to read what they have known into the text of the new book. So differences that are obvious to the specialist are not usually seen by the average parishioner until they are pointed out to him and carefully explained.

The fact that there has not been a greater outcry from clergy and laity concerning this revision of doctrine now written into the new liturgies probably is best explained in terms of a changing context. In the universities and seminaries, the older view of doctrine and the pursuit of theology as deduction from Scripture and tradition has gradually been giving way to new views that claim to be in tune with modern ways of study and in harmony with the scientific spirit. In 1970 one of my teachers, the late Professor Ian Ramsey of Oxford University, claimed that "theology is at present in turmoil. . . . Theology seems often to the outsider just so much word-spinning, airborne discourse which never touches down except disastrously" (*Models for Divine Activity*, 1973, 1). In a similar fashion and writing about the same time, Paul L. Holmer, professor of theology at Yale, spoke of the loss of control and authority in theology by such churches as the Roman Catholic, the Anglican, the Lutheran, and the Reformed or Presbyterian.

> In the name of theology, there is now a vast array of teachings, not quite in agreement with one another, but all of them bidding for attention within these groups. It is very hard, indeed, to make sense of it all. Theology looks almost promiscuous even where confessional views, Biblical allegiance and Christian authority are loudly asserted. For even these time-honored safeguards and criteria have been caught up in the whirl of ideas that counts as theology. (*The Grammar of Faith*, 1978, 1-2)

Then, also, major changes had been taking place in the general culture, especially in and from the 1960s, and ordinary parishioners had been gaining a modern mind-set, without perhaps realizing that their thinking patterns were being molded by the powerful winds of modernity. These winds at least conditioned them to turn inward and look for God more in present feelings and personal experience than in the transcendent, objective nature of majestic worship or in the disciplines of Bible study and self-denial. (In chapter four we shall be paying particular attention to the effect of the 1960s on the Christian faith.)

If we focus our attention on the new prayer books being used by Anglicans in North America, we find that there are three we have to consider. In the Episcopal Church (ECUSA) there is *The Book of Common Prayer* (1979) that is now the official book; this is supplemented by a book of trial liturgies, widely used and known as *Prayer Book Studies, 30* (1990). In the ECUSA the latest edition of the traditional prayer book was

1928, and this was the official book until it was replaced by the very different 1979 book.

Turning to Canada, we find that the latest edition of the traditional book was 1962 and that their new book, similar to the American 1979 book, is called *The Book of Alternative Services* (1985). Both books are used in Canada, but there is a very definite move by the majority of the bishops to persuade congregations to use the new book.

In my recently published study of the new liturgies, I have attempted to show that alongside a certain respect for the traditional services and doctrines, the current prayer books contain new doctrines of the Trinity, of the person and work of Christ, of the nature of man and his sin, of salvation, and of Scripture. They also show a growing readiness to use inclusive language both in the translation of sacred Scripture and in the provision of prayers and praises. For details I must invite my reader to see my book *Proclaiming the Gospel Through the Liturgy: The Common Prayer Tradition and Doctrinal Revision* (1993), along with its predecessor, *Knowing God Through the Liturgy* (1992).

Perhaps I can most easily bring to the surface the new theology, informing liturgical revision not only in Anglicanism but also through the whole ecumenical movement, if I set it out in terms of a 1 through 5. This way my reader can quickly and easily compare the theological foundation of classical Anglicanism with that of modern Anglicanism.

The original 1 through 5 (as I set it out above) appeared to last until recent times. In fact it survived in structure but not in content. Although the Bible remained the Bible with its two testaments, it was gradually viewed differently. It was studied via the developing historical-critical method; and while this brought benefits, it also tended to make the Bible into the inspired words of men about God rather than words inspired by God concerning God and His relationship to man. Also, while the creeds were retained, the Nicene and Athanasian were seen as containing what scholars were calling the hellenization of doctrine. That is, in their presentation of the dogma of the Holy Trinity and of the person of Jesus Christ it was judged that they contained Greek philosophical concepts (e.g., one substance) and so were not appropriate statements of faith for modern man. Further, it was held that the onward movement of historical research raised a whole series of questions concerning the viability of building a doctrinal structure on either the theology of the early centuries or of the Reformation.

Modern Anglicanism (like Lutheranism, Presbyterianism, Roman Catholicism, and Methodism) has intermarried with the family of theologies we know as nineteenth-century liberal theology and its modern developments (for that see the next chapter). The way it is heading now in terms of the contents of its prayer books (which provide the clearest evidence of the general effect of modern theology on the church) may be described as: (1) experience as the one and only foundation; (2) experience, however, of two kinds—that recorded in the Bible and in Christian history, and that which we enjoy today; (3) the third century after Christ as the century offering most guidance to us today; (4) benefiting from four revolutions; and (5) making available five or more (a plurality of) forms of worship.

Experience, the Only Foundation

We are dealing here with a very large and broad foundation. Personal experience originates in an encounter with the world, other persons, and one's own self. Further, such experience is continuous, and so what you or I experience now is affected in one degree or another by previous experience yesterday or the days before. Experience obviously includes the various reports of the five senses as well as basic feelings, attitudes, moods, and bodily expressions. Then also, there is a common and shared experience, so that people claim a common experience and are drawn together because of it—e.g., an association of families who have suffered and do still suffer the pain of having lost children through drugs and wish to help each other.

Added to direct personal experience, there is the study of human beings as experiencing persons. Such study can be of their inner life (psychology), their social relations and context (sociology), their communal practices and customs (anthropology), and their physiological, animal state (biology). Increasingly over the last century, experience has had the meaning of "observation of facts and events as a source of knowledge."

So it is not surprising that for liberal Christianity experience (personal, social, and from empirical study) has been and is understood as a medium of disclosure about the nature of the world as well as that which is "beyond" it. Additionally, since experience is many-sided and multi-relational, results and findings from aesthetics as well as science, ethics as well as economics, and religious as well as secular studies are all considered.

In the most basic sense it may be claimed that experience is the many-sided product of complex encounters between what there is and beings capable of undergoing, enduring, taking note of, responding to, and expressing this product. Moreover, such experience is the result of an ongoing process since our experiences are not isolated but are related to what has gone before. Finally, this approach to experience includes but is far more than what traditionally has been called religious experience. Anyone who carefully studies the new experimental services of the Episcopal Church found in *Prayer Book Studies, 30* will see how contemporary experience in the world is making its mark on theology and worship. What used to be seen as the influence of the world, the flesh, and the devil is now beginning to be seen as the presence and work of the Holy Spirit of God.

Biblical and Post-Biblical Experience

Liberal Protestantism has consistently taught that the Bible is the inspired record of the religious experience of Israel, Jesus, and the apostles of Jesus. That is, it is not (as orthodox Protestantism had claimed) the words of God in the words of men, but it is rather the words of men about their experience of God. As such, the Scriptures are precious and indispensable, though the sacred books do not give us revealed teaching from

God. It is the work of the contemporary theologian to use the record of the experience of God in the Old and New Testaments as the basis for his own reflection today, using the inductive and empirical method rather than the old, deductive method of pre-Enlightenment days.

As greater thought has been given to this approach since the 1960s, it has been pointed out (by feminists and others) that the experience recorded in the Bible is primarily the experience of males, written by males. In other words, it probably (certainly?) suffers from the diseases of patriarchalism, androcentricism, and sexism, for it was written in a male-dominated society for the benefit of males! Therefore, it has to be studied and used with great care by those who want to produce a liberated and just society. Even so, it is valuable if for no other reason than that it is primary—without it there would be no record of the origins of the Christian religion.

So, there is biblical experience. Since the writing of the New Testament there also has been a continuing stream of what can be called *religious* experience. This is recorded in a variety of sources from liturgical texts through autobiographical statements to books on prayer and spirituality. In the holy tradition of the church a claimed experience of God is channeled into specific rituals (forms of worship), celebrations (festival days), and ascetic duties (e.g., the keeping of Lent). Within specific types of Christianity (e.g., Anglican, Roman Catholic, and Lutheran) there has been a specific tradition of worship and spirituality in which it has been recognized that the faithful will have had an experience of God. Such religious experience is another source for theology; but here again there is the problem that much of it was written by males for males and from within patriarchal and racist societies.

Thus, the claim is made today that it is necessary for the modern theologian to add to what can be learned of God from the religious experience recorded in the Bible and available through the traditions of the church. What she or he must add is the study of experience that is not flawed through being interpreted through a patriarchalist and sexist bias. We find, for example, that the testimony of minorities (or of women) to discrimination and deprivation becomes an important source for modern theological reflection. It is hardly surprising, then, that conclusions drawn from the study of selected contemporary experience are often given preference over clear teachings found in the New Testament. For example, it is often said today that a homosexual relationship is acceptable to God if the couple remain faithful to each other. Such a statement flies in the face of the teaching of both the Old and New Testaments on sexual morality if that teaching is taken at its face value.

A few moments of reflection will lead one to see that once experience becomes the basis for theology, there can be a spectrum of possibilities from the conservative to the radical. Theology can then be constructed by an inductive method from:

> 1. The record of religious experience in the Bible.
> 2. The record of religious experience in the Bible and in holy tradition (or in a part thereof).
> 3. The record of religious experience in the Bible, Christian tradition, and the other theistic religions of the world (Islam and Judaism).
> 4. The record of religious experience in the Bible, Christian tradition, and all the religions of the world.
> 5. The record of religious experience (from all religions) and the study of the modern experience of women and/or minorities, as well as the reception of the "assured results" of study from the sociological and behavioral sciences concerning the nature and needs of human beings.

Originally, in the nineteenth century (as we shall see), liberal theology worked from numbers 1 and 2, but in recent times such combinations as numbers 4 and 5 have become common. That is, modern theologians tend to choose from the vast possibilities of total experience those aspects that further their position and cause. (See also below chapter six, "The Inductive Approach.")

An indication of how this approach has entered the Anglican

tradition of theology is best illustrated by reference to what has often been called the three-legged stool. Since the late-sixteenth century, the basis of the Anglican Way has been explained in terms of a commitment to the authority of the Holy Scriptures (see numbers 1 and 2 above), to tradition (see numbers 3, 4, and 5 above), and to reason (sanctified reason seeking to make clear to any one generation what the Lord God has revealed and taught to His church). In recent decades there has been talk of a four-legged stool, with the fourth leg being, at first, specifically religious experience and then, more recently, such human experience as had a bearing on modern religion. Thus, instead of the Bible's and traditional theology's judging contemporary ideas of religion, morality, and spirituality through rational study, the authority of modern experience invades and virtually takes over the exercise, and the three-legged becomes not a four-legged but in fact a one-legged stool!

The preface to the new Canadian Anglican prayer book of 1985, the *Book of Alternative Services*, tells how experience was a major factor in the creation of the new services. Writing in 1981 of the influences on those who created the new American Episcopal prayer book of 1979, the then dean of the University of the South at Sewanee, Dr. Urban T. Holmes, wrote:

> The new prayer book has, consciously or unconsciously, come to emphasize that understanding of the Christian experience that one might describe as a postcritical apprehension of symbolic reality and life in the community. It is consonant with Ricoeur's "second naivete," and is more expressive of Husserl, Heidegger, Otto, and Rahner than Barth or Brunner. (*Worship Points the Way*, 137)

One does not need to know anything about the European philosophers and theologians on this list to gain the impression that they were not the ones supportive of traditional orthodoxy.

As we shall see later in this book, Karl Rahner is the German Catholic theologian whose transcendental method has done much to change the traditional neo-Thomism or neo-Scholasticism of the Roman Catholic Church and open the doors to pluralism in theology. Rahner's many books were avidly read by leading American Episcopalians in the 1960s and 1970s. Even as Rahner made use of the existentialist philosophy of Martin Heidegger, so a leading Episcopal theologian, John MacQuarrie, translated the major work of Heidegger, *Being and Time*, and in the early 1960s published his own existentialist theology based on Heidegger, entitled *The Principles of Christian Theology*. This textbook was widely used in Episcopal seminaries for twenty years or so. In contrast, the two names that are set aside, Karl Barth and Emil Brunner (to whom we turn in the next chapter), were the heralds and the exponents of the new orthodoxy (neo-orthodoxy) of the twentieth century. Barth ranks as one of the greatest of Western theologians of all time. It was Barth and Brunner and others (as we shall see in chapter two) who led the movement away from the liberal theology that had dominated academic theology from the middle of the nineteenth century.

Perhaps I should add that in the middle years of the twentieth century, existentialism and personalism were the two preferred philosophies. Existentialism, as expounded by Martin Heidegger, for example, raised questions concerning human life that could be called religiously relevant; Karl Rahner made much use of it in his interpretation of Catholic theology. Personalism, as expounded by Martin Buber, for example, emphasized the fact that human personality, the I, is the most important phenomenon in this world. Brunner's neo-orthodoxy is heavily dependent on this personalism. There was also great interest in hermeneutics—the philosophical investigation of the process of interpretation of texts and of religious symbolism. Paul Ricoeur, along with Hans-Georg Gadamer, were the leading lights in this task. The "second naivêté" of Ricoeur points to a sophisticated understanding of traditional truths (e.g., the virginal conception of Jesus by Mary) in terms of non-literal but symbolic truth.

The Third Century

Within the Anglican Church, with its traditional liturgy that had been in use since 1549, those who wanted to introduce theological changes through liturgy had to find a different structure for the services into which they could introduce new doctrine. However, this structure had to be from the past, and preferably from the patristic era, in order to satisfy the inherent Anglican appeal to history. Thus the appeal to the third century—an appeal that was made also by Roman Catholic scholars during and after the Second Vatican Council (1962-65). This century was the period when the church was in (it was claimed) the multicultural, pluralistic culture of the Roman Empire and when there was flexibility with regard to both doctrinal statements and liturgical forms. This was also the period when the church was free of state control; it was not until after Constantine the Great became emperor early in the fourth century that Christianity became a lawful and then a preferred religion of the Roman Empire. So this was the period, it was claimed, most like the modern West, and thus the one to look to for inspiration!

Looking back to the church of the third century (of which our knowledge is minimal and hazy), liturgists produced new structures for the Eucharist and then filled the structures with a mixture of traditional and modern doctrine. They were able to introduce the new teaching because, having chosen a point in history before the ecumenical councils and before the development of dogma in the fourth and fifth centuries, they were set free from that classical teaching. In his book *Rites for a New Age* (1986), commending the new Canadian prayer book, Michael Ingham makes much of the similarity between the culture of the Roman Empire in the third and fourth centuries and that of North America today. Further, the leader of the liturgical revision in the Episcopal Church, Massey H. Shepherd Jr., wrote an essay in 1980 to point out that the 1979 book was based on this appeal to the third century (*The Historical Magazine of the Protestant Episcopal Church*, vol. 53, 221-234).

Four Revolutions

The doctrinal content of the new prayer books has been filtered through at least four revolutions. First, since it is in the language of the people and is a rejection of Western medieval ways, it has obviously come through the Protestant Reformation. In the second place it has come through the Enlightenment of the eighteenth century, for it is theology that begins with man (humankind) and works from man to God, rather than from God's self-revelation to man. It is basically a theology "from below" rather than a theology "from above." It begins from man's experience rather than from God's self-revelation.

Third, it has come through that so-called liberal or modernist theology (based on experience—as explained above) that has characterized liberal Protestantism since the nineteenth century, beginning with the seminal work of Friedrich Schleiermacher (see chapters two and six). A careful study of the catechism in the American 1979 prayer book will quickly confirm the observation that the theology has come via liberal theology. For example, the catechism begins with talk of human nature (not of the self-revealing God), and there is a rejection of the doctrine of original sin (i.e., as sickness and disease of the soul) in favor of seeing sin only as the abuse of freedom.

Finally, it has participated in the revolution that followed the Second Vatican Council. That council opened windows through which blew a mighty gale to dislodge traditional doctrine and liturgy and make space for innovations in both theology and liturgy. (For further details I commend Klaus Gamber, 1993.) Anyone who compares the new Anglican liturgies with those of the Roman Catholic Church will see many similarities. Moreover, when the modern are compared with the premodern, many major differences not only of structure but also in doctrine will be seen.

Five Eucharistic Prayers

In the traditional *Books of Common Prayer* from 1549 to 1962 there was always only one liturgical form for the administration of the Lord's Supper, the service of Holy Communion. The point of this was to present the most excellent form possible for universal use so that there was unity not only in spirit but also in thought and words in the church. This had the advantage that wherever the Anglican traveled and went to divine service he felt at home. In the new books there are at least five and often more such liturgical forms. In addition, there is the proviso that more such forms of service can be constructed to fit local conditions and desires.

Diversity is justified on the dubious basis that before the fourth century of the Christian era there was variety and not uniformity among churches. It is also justified on the basis of meeting modern needs, allowing a local congregation to choose what it thinks best serves its own particular situation. I might also add that diversity keeps the liturgists in business, for there is, in principle, no limit to the possibilities of new forms. It also means that the principle of relativism is built into this approach to worship, for one form is said to be as good as another, and what serves best is that which is felt to be right and appropriate in any given place at any specific time. Thereby, not only the principle of excellence but also the principle of authoritative, revealed doctrine is lost.

Perhaps now the claim of the modern liturgical movement both in Protestantism and Roman Catholicism and through ecumenism (the World Council of Churches) that the *lex orandi* (the law of praying) is the *lex credendi* (the law of believing) can be seen for what it is. Via the new liturgies, which contain new doctrine, major changes in what the church believes, teaches, and confesses are being introduced. People are participating in new liturgies that still use the language of Zion, and thereby they are receiving into their minds and hearts a new theology—even perhaps a new religion. Such a route is probably a more effective one for the entrance of modernity into the liturgical churches than any other!

Modern liturgists are not, however, content merely to create the law of believing through their law of praying. They want also to proclaim that the only valid, primary theology is theology that is based upon the liturgy; thus we hear a lot about liturgical theology. Also, as the experience of the last decade has shown, the so-called liturgical theology of the law of praying is also easily adaptable to become the vehicle for the expression of the modern theologies of ecology, feminism, liberation, and equal rights for any self-proclaimed, disadvantaged group.

Why do these churches emphasize the Eucharist so much when they apparently do not want to make much of the sacrificial death of Jesus? The answer comes in terms of the celebration of community. The coming together of individuals to form a community of celebration and to share a symbolic, common meal seems to be the major theme of the modern Eucharists. The emphasis is not upon the encounter with, and feeding by, the heavenly Christ who comes to His people who are gathered in His name as the Lord of glory; rather, it is upon the discovery of God's presence in and with those who come together to celebrate and affirm each other. This is why so much is made of the so-called peace—the greeting of each other by hugs and handshakes. Obviously, such an understanding and practice harmonizes with an experiential theology (numbers 1 and 2 above) and to a doctrine of God who is primarily, if not wholly, the immanent (in contrast to the transcendent) God.

Hopefully this presentation of the differences between classical or traditional Anglicanism and modern or contemporary Anglicanism will prepare the reader for what is to follow in the rest of the book. There appears to be a massive gap—symbolized by the Grand Canyon—between the method and ethos of theology in the sixteenth century and those of recent decades.

FOR FURTHER READING

The Book of Alternative Services of the Anglican Church of Canada. Toronto: The Anglican Book Center, 1985.

The Book of Common Prayer . . . of the Church of England

(1662). Cambridge, Mass.: Cambridge University Press, 1955.

The Book of Common Prayer (1928) . . . *of the Protestant Episcopal Church in the United States of America*. New York: Church Hymnal Corporation, 1928.

The Book of Common Prayer (1979) . . . *of the Episcopal Church*. New York: Seabury, 1979.

Gamber, Klaus. *The Reform of the Roman Liturgy: Its Problems and Background*. San Juan Capistrano, Calif.: Una Voce Press, 1993.

Holmes, Urban T. "Education for Liturgy." In *Worship Points the Way*. Edited by Malcolm C. Burson. New York: Seabury, 1981.

Toon, Peter. *Knowing God Through the Liturgy*. Largo, Fla.: Prayer Book Publishing Company, 1992.

_____. *Proclaiming the Gospel Through the Liturgy*. Largo, Fla.: Prayer Book Publishing Company, 1993.

_____. *Which Rite Is Right? The Eucharistic Prayer in the Anglican Tradition*. Swedesboro, N.J.: Preservation Press, 1994.

Chapter 2

Heredity: Liberal Theology and Its Children

Liberal theology is a cluster or family of theologies that originated in Europe in the confidence of the early nineteenth century. It was the theology of liberal Protestantism. That is, it was an accommodation of the teaching of historical Protestantism (e.g., Lutheranism) to an increasingly scientific and secularist age. It was motivated by a deep sense of the need to adapt the received faith to the intellectual, social, and moral needs of the new epoch in Western history. To use the analogy of a family (as developed by the late Dr. Henry P. Van Dusen), liberal theology was the offspring of two nineteenth-century parents. In this marriage of ideas, one parent was the new intellectual outlook of that age that had emerged from the European Enlightenment. The chief mark of this outlook was a new confidence in the power of reason to discover truth. The way to find things out, it was claimed, was not by believing what someone else in authority said, but by considering the evidence, reflecting on it, and accepting only what could be proved at the bar of reason. The other parent was the genuine religious resurgence of that period (in contrast to the general lack of religious vitality in the European churches of the late eighteenth century). Yet, as we will see, a major casualty of this marriage was the gradual erosion of the notion of doctrine as a body of authoritative teaching that prescribed and explained what the Christian faith means and demands of believers.

THE ADAM AND EVE OF PROTESTANT LIBERALISM

From the one parent, whom we will designate as the male, came two basic endowments. The first was an intellectual perspective expressed in an openness to receiving new truth from experimental and empirical science. With this went a critical approach to the historical documents, holy traditions, and the varied legacy of Christendom. The second endowment was a basic theoretical assumption that there is a continuity between special revelation, recorded in the Bible, and natural revelation, known by the inductive method from the study of the cosmos. Connected with this there is also a basic relation with, rather than opposition among, Christianity and other religions, for all religion is the interpretation of claimed experience of the supernatural or the divine.

Thus, the characteristics of the endowments from the "father" included faithfulness to the truth wherever the truth led, deference to the findings of theoretical and empirical science, commitment to the historical-critical method in the study of the Bible and Christian literature, and a tentativeness as to the certainty of any knowledge belonging to the field of metaphysics (that which is above and beyond the natural world). Religiously, this meant that God was more likely to be sought as the unifier of the universe than as above and beyond the universe; thus there was an emphasis on the immanence rather than the transcendence of God.

From the other parent, whom we will designate as the female, also came two basic endowments. The first was a spiritual vitality and power, expressed in lofty ideals, moral consciousness, and a sense of unity with the spiritual wisdom and moral achievements of the past. The second was a central and regnant conviction that the Jesus of history, known by historical research, and the living Christ of today, known in religious experience and in Christian worship, are a single organic, indissoluble, personal reality.

Thus, the characteristics of the endowments from the "mother" pertained to the authority of religious experience in its subjective, individualistic, and spiritual reality as the presence of God, the living Christ, in the souls of believers. Parallel to this was commitment to the humanity of Jesus, to the so-called historical Jesus, to His personality and teaching, to the finding and knowing of His God as a kind father, and to the treating of fellow human beings as brothers and sisters.

The offspring of this union also inherited a conscious rejection of what seemed to them to be a spiritually barren, even dead, Protestant orthodoxy in either its Reformed or Lutheran form. New wine could not be kept in old wineskins. This meant the setting aside of traditional metaphysical assumptions (e.g., the claimed knowledge of God-as-God-is-in-Himself; the Blessed Trinity of the Father, the Son, and the Holy Spirit; and His eternal attributes), and the adoption of seemingly practical doctrines (e.g., knowledge of God-as-God-is-toward-us, around and within us). It also meant the bringing of what had been previously known as the inspired, infallible Bible to the bar of the judgment of reason; here it was deemed to be not the Word of God in the words of men, but the words of men describing their experience of God. Human experience of God, rather than a claimed self-revelation by God, then became the basis for theological reflection in the faculties of theology. Within the churches, the slogan "life, not doctrine" communicated the priority of activity over study and inner experience over doctrinal norm.

These confident offspring were affected by the Enlightenment, Romanticism, and Pietism because they emphasized rationality, feeling, and genuine religion. In their genes were the inheritance of the philosophy of Immanuel Kant (1724-1804), the great thinker that we associate with the Enlightenment, and the insights and feelings of the first great modern theologian, Friedrich Schleiermacher (1768-1834) of Berlin. In Schleiermacher we encounter both a response to the Enlightenment and the mood of Romanticism in (what he judged to be) the service of Jesus Christ—and all this from a personal background within Pietism.

Schleiermacher is rightly called the father of modern or liberal theology. In brief, he held that religion is of the heart, the feeling of absolute dependence on God, and that in Christianity the religious purpose is to experience that same dependence on God that Jesus Himself experienced. In fact, it is the extent of Jesus' God-consciousness and His perfect realization of the human ideal that sets Him apart from other men and makes Him the Savior, for His disciples are to seek to experience that consciousness of God that He experienced in fullness. Thus, the church is that part of mankind that participates in and also shares the Christian consciousness. Theology is an ordered account and interpretation of religious experience—a task done brilliantly by Schleiermacher in his *Christian Faith: Presented in Its Inner Connections According to the Fundamentals of the Evangelical Church* (1830).

In this book, Schleiermacher attempts to show that true religion is neither knowing nor doing but is operative at a deeper level of the soul. In his propositions 3 and 4 he wrote:

> The piety which forms the basis of all ecclesiastical communions is, considered purely in itself, neither a Knowing nor a Doing, but a modification of Feeling, or of immediate self-consciousness.
>
> The common element in all howsoever diverse expressions of piety by which these are conjointly distinguished from all other feelings, or, in other words, the self-identical essence of piety, is this: the consciousness of being absolutely dependent, or, which is the same thing, of being in relation to God.

At the very center or core of the human being there is a religious awareness. In other words, a self-awareness, at its deepest level, involves both awareness of human finitude and of the infinity (God) on which human beings depend. So one can say that the basis of all human experience is truly religious experience.

Much earlier in his *On Religion: Speeches to Its Cultured Despisers* (1799), Schleiermacher described this immanent, human spirituality (which in Kantian terms could be called transcendental) in these glowing terms:

> The man who does not see miracles of his own from the standpoint from which he contemplates the world; the man in whose heart no revelation of his own arises when his soul longs to draw in the beauty of the world and to be permeated by its spirit; the man who does not, in supreme moments, feel with the most lively assurance, that a divine spirit urges him, and that he speaks and acts from holy inspiration, has no religion. (1958 ed., 90)

So, true religion should be acceptable to the highest human culture, for it blesses and enhances the soul.

Kant claimed to present a critical philosophy that gave a rightful place to the emerging natural science and that preserved a sphere for religion and the good life flowing from it. It has been said of him that he is the last great thinker in whom the Western mind is held together. Kant proposed that knowledge and belief be seen as two different mental activities. Knowledge, as the possession of science, is gained by the study of the phenomenal world with its observable data and its rationally grounded laws. However, this world can neither be the basis for faith nor an effective obstacle to faith. Natural science has its sphere and validity, and this is the exercise of pure reason; but it has nothing to say concerning the moral and spiritual life of man.

The latter sphere belongs to the exercise of the practical reason where belief is appropriate. Man has a spiritual nature, and as a spiritual being he believes that there is a transcendental world of spirit and freedom that pure reason and knowledge cannot reach. Yet, man cannot speak of this spiritual realm except through symbolism, because he has no knowledge of it;

he only has the sense of and belief in this noumenal world, which is a sufficient basis for religious faith. So we see that Kant appeared to make room for both the advance of the sciences and the practice of religion. As we noted with Schleiermacher, however, theology became the study of the belief and experience of the Christian church, not the claim to discuss knowledge of God given by God in self-revelation.

After Kant and Schleiermacher, anyone who sought to do theology in what can be called a pre-modern mode and to treat the Bible as the source of true propositions concerning both God-as-God-is-in-Himself and God-as-God-is-toward-us was to be out of the intellectual mainstream of Protestant thought and theology. It was to swim against the tide. Of course there were those, especially in the parishes and in the new evangelical movements of the nineteenth century, who did swim against the tide and sought to keep alive the older Protestant ways of doing theology. Yet even here there was a tendency to be deeply affected by the cultivation of what John Wesley called experimental religion (the inner experience). There were also those who sought to swim with the tide, seeking not to be overwhelmed by its force, as well as those who swam with the tide, seeking not to be driven too forcefully by it.

Outside Protestantism, within the Roman Catholic seminaries and universities, as well as in Greece and Russia, theology generally continued as it had before the Enlightenment. The winds blowing through Protestantism in the nineteenth century did not really get to blow through Roman Catholicism and Orthodoxy until the twentieth century.

For those in the early nineteenth century who had come through the Enlightenment or lived in its atmosphere, there was another alternative route to that of Kant via Schleiermacher and into liberal theology. This was to follow in the philosophical ways of Georg W. F. Hegel (1770-1831), who taught in Berlin at the same time as Schleiermacher. His was the route of idealist philosophy, which as an intellectual movement persisted into the early twentieth century. While Schleiermacher sought to secure in his theology the uniqueness of Christian faith (the experience of believing), Hegel attempted to ground or embed the faith in the cosmic movement of reason. His motto was: "The real is the rational and the rational is the real." To this extent he was very close to the Enlightenment. Hegel, however, also had a high regard for history, and he succeeded in incorporating the new historical consciousness of the early nineteenth century into his theology.

The idealism that Hegel taught is absolute because he saw all reality as gathered up into the all-embracing, all-encompassing, impersonal Mind/Spirit, or *Geist*, which is God. Further, in all reality (both physical and mental/spiritual), he saw a particular rhythm or pattern of movement of three stages that he called dialectic. This is the movement from a starting-point (the thesis) to another point (the antithesis), which is over against or opposed to the initial point. Finally, there is the reconciliation and reintegration of the thesis and antithesis at a higher level in what he called the synthesis. This rational dialectic was a restatement of a favorite theme of the Romantic movement (which affected Hegel as well as Schleiermacher), known as the coincidence of opposites. By this theory the Romantics sought to escape from the older rationalist insistence on the law of non-contradiction and allow for the discovery of the new—the interplay of opposites and the connection between the whole and the part, the inner and the outer, the individual and the universal.

In Hegel's system, the coincidence of opposites occurred as dialectic spoke eloquently of a total system of the movement of God as *Geist* through projection (thesis producing antithesis) and its return as synthesis. Thus, the Trinity is this threefold, universal dialectic process, and the doctrines of creation and incarnation are the antithesis produced by *Geist*—the thesis in its self-projection as Nature.

Moreover, the Hegelian dialectic contributed to the growing awareness of, and appreciation for, history. It made this contribution by providing a means for understanding history as a dynamic process of struggle, conflict, and risk as it moved toward a greater or higher end. Not surprisingly, therefore, Hegel's philosophy gave a strong impetus to the study of Christian origins and the history of the development of theology and Christian thought.

Hegel had many disciples who may be said to belong to the right and left wings of Hegelianism. The right wing consists of those who sought to develop his philosophy of absolute idealism, among whom are some distinguished British names— Edward Caird, F. H. Bradley, Josiah Royce, A. S. Pringle-Pattison, and J. M. McTaggart. The left includes those who used parts of his philosophy for particular ends—e.g., Ludwig Feuerbach, Karl Marx, and Søren Kierkegaard. Also, his concept of dialectic was used for historical study by some radical German New Testament scholars—e.g., F. C. Baur and D. F. Strauss. (Those who have read C. S. Lewis's autobiography *Surprised by Joy* [1955] will recall that he was attracted by idealism as taught by Bradley in the 1920s before becoming a theist.)

Looking over to Europe from Britain in 1857 when liberal theology was beginning to be in full flow in Germany, Mark Pattison wrote:

> It must not be supposed that German Theology is some obscure national product, the concern exclusively of the country that has given it birth. It is no insulated phenomenon. Though generated in Germany, it belongs to Christendom. It is the theological movement of the age. It is only because there is fuller intellectual life in Germany than elsewhere— only because it so happens that, at present, European speculation is transacted by Germans, as our financial affairs by Jews—that German characteristics are impressed on the substance of the Christian science. The capital of learning is in the hands of Germans, and theirs has been the enterprise which has directed it into theological channels. (Cited by H. R. Mackintosh, 1937, 3)

We may recall that Germany at that time had twenty-five university faculties of theology that enjoyed wide doctrinal freedom and that belonged to an academia that had a love of thorough and exact knowledge. A defect of German theology, however, was its lack of vital contact with the worship and witness of the faithful in the parishes.

ADAM AND EVE'S CHILDREN

To find influential examples of these offspring who lived in the atmosphere created by the teaching of Kant, Hegel, and Schleiermacher, one need only study the writings and encounter the theology of such German theologians as Albrecht Ritschl (1822-89), the founder of the liberal Protestant school and his disciples, Johann Wilhelm Herrman (1846-1922) of Marburg, Julius Kaftan (1848-1926) of Berlin, and Adolf von Harnack (1851-1930), also of Berlin. We shall notice only Ritschl and Harnack. Behind and through their creative and brilliant writings several basic Christian doctrines were abandoned (e.g., that of original sin) and others were reinterpreted (e.g., Christology, the identity of Jesus Christ).

Ritschl was a professor in Göttingen beginning in 1864, from where he launched what was initially called Ritschlian theology but is now more usually called liberal theology. He was heavily dependent on Kant for his emphasis both on the kingdom of God and moral experience and the unknowableness of ultimate reality. He adopted Kant's doctrine of practical reason. His major work in restating Protestant doctrine was *The Christian Doctrine of Justification and Reconciliation*, published in three volumes between 1870 and 1874, of which only the first and third were translated into English. The first volume was a historical survey of the doctrines, the second was an exposition of biblical material, and the third attempted a reconstruction of the doctrines in terms of Christian experience of the grace of God.

In the latter Ritschl argued that the purpose of the Christian religion is not to enjoy a mystical communion with God (who is unknowable) but rather to overcome by divine grace and with moral virtue the contradictions that run through human existence. His own definition of Christianity, which he saw as a recovery and purification of the Lutheran view, was:

> Christianity is the monotheistic, completely spiritual and eth-
> ical religion, which, on the basis of the life of its Founder
> [Jesus Christ] as redeeming and establishing the kingdom of
> God, consists in the freedom of the children of God, includes
> the impulse to conduct from the motive of love, the intention
> of which is the moral organisation of mankind; and in the fil-
> ial relation to God as well as in the kingdom of God lays the
> foundation of blessedness. (3:13)

The twin themes of spiritual redemption in Jesus and moral endeavor in the ethical community, the church, constitute the Christian faith as an ellipse with two foci, rather than as a circle with a single center. Christians do not know God as God; they only know the blessings and the benefits that God's presence and grace bring. Thus Ritschl's theology remains, as with Schleiermacher's, experience-theology; reflection not on God as the God who reveals Himself to man, but on claimed experience of God.

Harnack was a professor at the University of Berlin beginning in 1889 and was known as a man of massive learning, a prolific author, a gifted lecturer, and a public figure with social prestige and influence. The academic study for which he is best known is his *History of Dogma*, first published in German between 1885 and 1888. He showed himself a Ritschlian by his thesis that the original Gospel of Jesus was soon overlaid by alien elements from Greek and Roman culture. It was his contention that the early Fathers, seeking to make the Gospel intelligible to the Greek-speaking world of the Roman Empire, actually changed it by interpreting it through Greek philosophical categories. At the same time, the organizing genius of the Roman Empire entered and organized what was originally a loose fellowship of congregations or a federation of churches into a centralized catholic church with a hierarchy, laws, and sacramental system. Thus it was, claimed Harnack, that living faith became a creed, devotion to Christ became Christology, ministers of the Spirit became clerics, and Christianity became ineffectual because it was overlaid with alien elements.

For Harnack, as for Ritschl, the Protestant Reformation was a move in the right direction, but it did not go far enough. Alien elements remained; thus it was the calling of liberal theology to remove these and restore the original gospel. So in 1899, exactly one hundred years after Schleiermacher's lectures in Berlin published as *On Religion: Speeches to Its Cultured Despisers*, Harnack gave sixteen lectures to students of the University of Berlin on the essence of the Gospel—that is, the meaning of the Gospel as set free from the accretions of the patristic and medieval eras. Later published in German in 1900 as *Das Wesen des Christentums* (The Essence of Christianity) and in English as *What is Christianity?* in 1901, these lectures spread the message far and wide as to what liberal theology understood by the essence of the Gospel.

It is unfair to Harnack to say that he saw the essence as the Fatherhood of God and the brotherhood of man. Certainly this is how many have interpreted what he and others said. However, what Harnack claimed was more subtle, and he preferred to summarize the teaching of Jesus as the kingdom of God and its coming; God the Father and the infinite value of the human soul; and the higher righteousness and the commandment of love. For Harnack the coming of the kingdom is the rule of God in the heart and is the possession of eternal life. Such a Christian life is lived in the knowledge that God is our Father, that His providence guides our lives and rules the world, and that we (believers) are His children, infinitely valuable in His sight.

Christianity is the religion *of* Jesus rather than the religion *about* Jesus, of whom Harnack wrote:

> That Jesus' message is so great and so powerful lies in the fact that it is so simple and on the other hand so rich; so simple as to be exhausted in each of the leading thoughts which he uttered; so rich that every one of these thoughts seems to be inexhaustible and the full meaning of the sayings and parables beyond our reach. But more than that—he himself stands behind everything that he said. His words speak to us across

> the centuries with the freshness of the present. (*What Is Christianity?*, 1958, 46)

The religion of Jesus is "eternal life in the midst of time, by the strength and under the eyes of God" (ibid., 18). The preaching of the Gospel is the communicating of the essence of the meaning of the life and teaching of Jesus in an appropriate, intelligible form.

Carl F. H. Henry, an evangelical who understands liberal theology, described its dominance at the close of the nineteenth century and in the first fifteen years of the twentieth century. He saw both the philosophical influence (via Hegel and idealistic philosophy) and the theological influence (via Ritschl and his school):

> The theology which captured the seminaries and universities, which seized the initiative in the publication of religious literature and the presentation of its viewpoint in the scholarly societies and journals, which came increasingly to control the machinery of the large denominations, and which was projected by many of the most active enthusiasts for world church unity, was rooted in the philosophies both of immanentism and evolutionism, and rejected the objective authority of the Scriptures, the necessity and possibility of miraculous revelation, and with these the biblical pattern of sin and redemption. Walter Marshall is surely right when he singles out the period from 1849 to 1914 as "the great age of liberalism." (*Fifty Years of Protestant Theology*, 30-31)

Henry insisted that by 1900 liberalism was a single movement, howbeit with many expressions, and that its chief foe was traditional orthodoxy (evangelical theology). Thus he wrote:

> In Germany, on the British Isles, in the United States, and elsewhere as well, it busied itself along identical lines: evangelical theology was proclaimed to be obscurantist and outmoded, liberalism had the scholarship and genius to restate Christianity definitively in modern categories. Biblical theology was being "remade" in terms of the modern mind. The determinative principles, inherited from the nineteenth century, were those of immanental and evolutionary philosophy,

with their rejection of special revelation, miracle, the unique deity of Christ, and a divinely ordered redemption, or in a summary word, the trustworthiness of the Bible. (*Fifty Years*, 32-33)

Henry well understood that at that time there seemed little or no reason to question the prevailing notions of man's natural perfectibility and the automatic advance of human history and civilization. This was because both of these concepts gained their cogency and attractiveness from idealist philosophy, with its teaching of the progressive externalization of the Absolute (God) in man and his future in space and time. These concepts also were (seemingly) confirmed by the way European civilization was advancing over the earth and scientific endeavor was mastering the elements of the world.

Writing before the First World War, the famous German theologian and missionary Albert Schweitzer had this to say about the quality of German theologians of the nineteenth century:

> When, at some future day, our period of civilization shall lie, closed and completed, before the eyes of later generations, German theology will stand out as a great, a unique phenomenon in the mental and spiritual life of our time. For nowhere save in the German temperament can there be found in the same perfection the living complex of conditions and factors—of philosophical thought, critical acumen, historical insight and religious feeling—without which no deep theology is possible. (*The Quest of the Historical Jesus*, German 1906, English 1911, 1)

In fact, Schweitzer's book was one of the causes that led to the collapse of liberal theology in Germany. This was because he cast doubt on the claim of the German theologians to objective, historical knowledge about Jesus (the Jesus of history).

LIBERAL THEOLOGY OUTSIDE GERMANY

This family of expressions of nonorthodox and nontraditional theologies called liberal theology reigned virtually supreme in the Protestant theology faculties of German universities up to the end of the First World War (1914-18). Then it was seriously challenged, went into decline, and was replaced by a new movement—a story we shall return to later.

For various reasons, the beginning of the demise of liberal theology in America came some twenty or so years later than in Europe. Until the 1930s it was dominant in most of the faculties of theology and seminaries in America belonging to the old-line churches. These were organized on the model of the faculty of theology in the German university with the separation of the various disciplines. And, as we would expect, this organization allowed for the dominance of post-Enlightenment thought and liberal theology. A much-used exposition by students was W. N. Clarke's *Outline of Christian Theology* (1898), and with this we should mention the writings of both H. C. King (1858-1934) and Shailer Matthews (1863-1941) of the Chicago school. The general character of American liberalism may be stated in terms of four basic affirmations.

First of all, American liberalism emphasized the importance of the inductive method of inquiry that had proven so successful in other fields for the study of religion. This had important consequences for the study of the Bible and meant the adoption not only of lower criticism (textual study) but also of higher criticism (the historical-critical method). Thus, the Bible was generally viewed as only the human witness of God, rather than the true Word of God in the words of men. From the perspective of ordinary parishioners, who received these new ideas as processed by the minds of their pastors, it seemed at times as if the Bible was a book primarily for scholars. Furthermore, much of what they thought was Christian had been based, it appeared, on imperfect study, faulty knowledge, and out-of-date cosmology. They had been given too much of the husk and not enough of the corn!

In the second place, there was the reliance on experience. Of course, this included the experience of people recorded in the Bible, and particularly the unique experience of Jesus; but it did not stop there, for it also included the experience of all

Christians through the centuries and in fact the whole of human life. To study and to arrange in order this large field of evidence, reason needed to step in. Each person needed to develop his own faith on the basis of personal experience, rather than on the dogmatic utterances of others. So, though the Bible had become a partly closed book for the laity, they now were encouraged to see Christianity in life rather than in doctrine and to find God at work in the movement of history and in their day-to-day experiences. Such a position fitted in well, of course, with the growing sense of individualism, both utilitarian and expressive, in Western society (for that see the next chapter).

In the third place, there was a great emphasis on the unity of truth about God and man. A continuity was thus claimed and seen between God and the human race, as well as between revelation and reason. To study human beings is also to study God, it was claimed. Such thinking was possible because liberals emphasized the immanence and omnipresence of God and said little about his transcendence and majesty. He was the God of space and time rather than the God above and beyond space and time. On this basis, the adoption of the theory of the evolution of the species came reasonably easily to liberals. They saw in it a confirmation of the continuity of the human race not only with the whole created order but also with God as present within the cosmos. At the parish level, especially as modern Western individualism steadily entered human consciousness and experience, the thought of the nearness of God as benevolent, uniting, and sustaining Spirit was attractive and supportive.

Finally, there was an optimistic estimate of human potential. If the social, physical, and economic environments were improved, then human beings would improve, and the social order would approximate more closely to the ideals of the kingdom of God. In fact, the strength of the social-gospel movement in America at the beginning of the twentieth century is a testimony to this optimism. No person so clearly stated its basis and goals as did Walter Rauschenbusch (1861-1918), the leading and articulate theologian of the social-gospel movement, who often quoted Ritschl. He believed that most human imperfections could be traced to the environment and that one generation of human beings corrupted the next. Society had to be remade, and he declared that we love and serve God when we love and serve our fellows, whom He loves and in whom He lives. His *Theology for the Social Gospel* (1917) is a moving plea that the Ritschlian idea of the kingdom of God become the controlling theme of Christian theology.

Outside the seminaries and universities, one of the most articulate and significant spokesmen for liberal theology was Harry Emerson Fosdick (1878-1969), pastor of Riverside Church, New York City. His preaching ministry there from 1930 to 1946 was one of the most, if not *the* most, influential in the United States because he spoke both to a vast congregation in person and to thousands more via the radio. He spoke against fundamentalism and obscurantism on the one side and against reducing the truths of Christianity to contemporary wisdom in the name of faith and reason on the other side. He attempted to present what he called the abiding truths of the faith in the changing categories appropriate for the modern world. His books of sermons and presentation of Christian liberalism presented liberal theology and a social gospel in simple and attractive terms. However, toward the end of his public ministry he did acknowledge that there were severe deficiencies in the liberal theology with which he had identified.

If we cross the ocean to Britain and look for an example of an attractive liberal theologian, we would probably choose John Oman (1860-1939), who taught at Westminster College in Cambridge and who sought to improve and extend what Schleiermacher had suggested. He did this through the use and development of the theme of personality—as in his book *Grace and Personality* (1917). Within the Church of England a group of liberals formed the Modern Churchman's Union. One of the most well-known members was Hastings Rashdall (1858-1924), author of *The Idea of Atonement in Christian Theology* (1919). In this book, he explained that the death of Jesus is only an example to us of divine love and is in no sense a sacrifice for the sin of the world. However, the way of the British theologians was generally to seek to steer a middle way between the old orthodoxy and the new liberal theology—as can be seen in the influential writings of William Temple (1881-1944), who became the Archbishop of Canterbury.

EVANGELICAL RESPONSE

Evangelicals in America recall that as early as 1923 J. Gresham Machen (1881-1937), representing what has been called the scholarship of consistent supernaturalism, published his attack on liberal theology, *Christianity and Liberalism.* As a Presbyterian evangelical who saw liberal theology infiltrating his own tradition and who had no interest in neo-orthodoxy, Machen demonstrated conclusively that the message of Protestant liberalism (which he took to be the general father-hood of God and the universal brotherhood of man) was not the Gospel of the New Testament. What Machen appears not to have seen as clearly perhaps as we can see today is that liberal theology had a fine aim—to make Christianity relevant to the changing intellectual and social scenes in the Western world. Certainly it must be judged to have failed in this aim, and what it offered as the Christian faith was at best a very diluted form of this faith.

Having mentioned evangelicals, it is perhaps appropriate here to recall the publication from 1910 of *The Fundamentals* in twelve volumes containing some ninety essays or articles. Sponsored by two wealthy businessmen, these tracts for the times were intended to check the advance of what was then called the new Christianity and the new theology (i.e., liberal Protestantism and its doctrines). Although they provided an excellent presentation of a wide evangelical consensus on basic doctrines and refutations of perceived errors and heresies, they served primarily to strengthen the evangelical cause and made little or no impact on the so-called new Christianity. It is not surprising, then, that this same period witnessed the gradual separation of a distinctive evangelical Protestantism from the dominant liberal Protestantism. The evangelical movement both stayed within the old-line churches and also moved outside them. It founded its own educational colleges and theological seminaries; but it also soon showed by its own internal divisions that it is all too easy, even for those who seek to be faithful to Scripture, to major on minors and thereby lose a basic unity.

Since the second decade of this century, the evangelical movement has remained a significant yet divided movement, with its members often attacking each other's theologies more enthusiastically than those of their opponents within the liberal camp. In addition, the movement, while enjoying a high profile on the American scene and criticizing the liberalism of the old-line churches, has also made significant accommodations to the spirit of secular modernity. These accommodations have been clearly explained by both James D. Hunter in his *American Evangelicalism: Conservative Religion and the Quandary of Modernity* (1983) and by David F. Wells in his *No Place for Truth: Or, Whatever Happened to Evangelical Theology?* (1993). In fact, the claim is sometimes heard today that some modern reforming evangelicals, who seek to have a relevant and definite social gospel for modern America, are in essence restoring the better insights of liberal theology. So it is said that they are the true heirs of the social-gospel movement of seventy years ago and that liberal theology is alive and well in left-wing evangelicalism.

Also, it is noteworthy that there has moved from liberal Protestantism to right-wing evangelicalism the torch of support for American democracy. A new alliance between the American experiment in democracy and right-wing evangelical religion was forged in the 1970s at the same time that the alienation of liberal Protestantism from American democratic faith was becoming apparent.

REBELLIOUS CHILDREN: THE RISE OF
NEO-ORTHODOXY

By 1950 the major question being asked by American theologians was not (as during the former liberal era), how can the Christian faith be made intelligible within, and in harmony with, the highest idealism and scientific thought of Western civilization? Rather, the question was, what is there in the Christian faith that gives us such an understanding of ourselves that we must assert our loyalty to the Holy God above all the splendid and yet corruptible values of Western civilization? The reason for the change of question may be traced primarily to one Swiss theologian, Karl Barth, and one movement, neo-orthodoxy.

The First World War (1914-18) seemed to shake the very foundations of the world for Europeans. Many of the leading liberal theologians had supported the war policy of the Kaiser in 1914 as necessary for the defense and maintenance of Christian civilization. But Barth, in his small Swiss parish of Safenwil, knew early in that cruel war that not only the political ideals but also the theology of his former teachers (e.g., Herrman and Harnack) had been shattered. The identification of Christianity with the best of German culture (what was called *Kulturprotestantismus*) was not only wrong, it was sinful.

Further, that other great theme of liberalism, *Ehrfurcht vor Geschichte* (reverence before history), also lost credibility. If there was progress through history, what kind of progress could be claimed from the carnage and devastation of the battlefields of this war? As a result, Barth and other young men rejected the liberal theology and began to look in other directions in their search for truth. Thus dialectical theology was born. Indeed, a sober estimate of human nature and human potential, together with an exalted view of the living, holy God, came from those whom we may call the rebellious grandchildren of the first parents.

Together with Barth, exponents of this rebellion against liberal theology included such well-known names as Emil Brunner (1889-1966), also from Switzerland, and the Germans Rudolf Bultmann (1884-1976) and Friedrich Gogarten (1887-1967). The leaders of this school spoke of a crisis, pointing to the *krisis* (Greek for "judgment") of God on mankind and its sinfulness. They also followed the Danish philosopher Kierkegaard in using the method of statement and counter-statement, never daring, as sinners who only knew God and His ways in part, to produce the last and final word. They were extremely conscious in their finitude of speaking of eternity and infinity and thus emphasized the need for dialectic. The theologian must speak God's yes as well as God's no and realize that while the opposites seem contradictory to us, they are not so to God Himself.

While the members of this school did not agree among themselves in all their positive proposals (and later parted company), they were of one mind in their decisive rejection of the central themes of liberal theology concerning human progress and perfectibility. However, in that they accepted the historical-critical method in their reading and use of the Bible (while having a very high view of the Bible as witnessing to God's self-revelation in Jesus Christ), their respective theologies showed themselves to be, under close examination, tied (at least in a minimal way) to the apron strings of their liberal parents.

From Barth came a sustained and massive effort to establish the utter transcendence and glory of God. He asserted that we know the Father only in the Lord Jesus Christ, who is the Incarnate Son and Word of the Father. He rejected all claims of continuity between natural theology and revealed theology; he would have nothing to do with the dissolving of the glorious transcendence and apartness of God into the immanence and omnipresence of God, which was so characteristic of liberal theology. In the preface to the second edition of his famous commentary on *The Epistle to the Romans* (1921), Barth spoke of his system in this manner:

> If I have a system, it is limited to a recognition of what Kierkegaard called the "infinite qualitative distinction

between time and eternity," and to my regarding this as pos-
sessing negative as well as positive significance: "God is in
heaven and thou art on earth." The relation between such a
God and such a man, and the relation between such a man and
such a God, is for me the theme of the Bible and the essence
of philosophy.

And at the meeting of God and man, man and God, is Jesus
Christ, who is the living Word of God. Any viable theology
must be built on Him, for only thereby can God be God unto
mankind.

Barth's commentary caused a sensation in Germany, arous-
ing both enthusiasm and hostility. Later Barth, who at this time
was pastoring in his native Switzerland, said he felt at that time
like a little urchin who had climbed up into the belfry of his local
church when everyone was asleep and had pulled on the rope
he found there—only to find that he had set the great bell in
motion, which awakened the whole parish. Certainly there was
fire in Barth's belly, but there was also thunder and lightning in
his words. The book served to be a launchpad for the new
movement called dialectical theology. The cry was: "Let God be
God." And for ten years or so Barth was a dialectical theologian.

Neo-orthodoxy had not yet been born. It had to wait for the
maturing of Barth's theology as he studied the Bible, the early
Fathers, Anselm of Canterbury, and other sources. It also had
to wait for his parting of the ways from Bultmann and
Gogarten, and to a much lesser degree from Brunner. We shall
encounter Bultmann's great influence later in our story (chapter four), since his major impact outside Germany on theology
was after the Second World War.

Barth's mature thought is to be found in his massive *Church
Dogmatics*, begun in 1932. Here is the new orthodoxy in that
the dialectic is much reduced and the biblical and patristic com-
ponents are greatly increased. The central focus of his attention
is Jesus Christ, the Word of God made flesh who dwelt among
us. Since Jesus is truly God and truly man, He is the mirror by
which we see who God is and what the nature of man is. Jesus

is also the key to understanding both the purpose of human existence and the creating, reconciling, revealing, and redeeming work of God. So neo-orthodoxy from Barth's pen is Christocentric. It involved a reworking and restating of the classic, patristic doctrine of the person of Christ (one person with two natures, as defined at the Council of Chalcedon and set forth in the Athanasian Creed); and it also involved a fresh statement of the "being" of God as "Father, Son and Holy Spirit."

Barth's friend and mentor, the Scottish theologian Thomas F. Torrance, wrote:

> Karl Barth has in fact so changed the whole landscape of theology, evangelical and catholic alike, that the other great theologians of modern times appear in comparison like jobbing gardeners. When Karl Barth died on December 10, 1968, I thought that we might well apply to him what Albert Einstein once wrote of Isaac Newton: "To think of him is to think of his work. For such a man can be understood only by thinking of him as a scene on which the struggle for eternal truth took place." That is surely what we must remember about Karl Barth, for in him there took place a profound struggle for the eternal Word of God in which the whole framework of the church's understanding of God from ancient to modern times was subjected to critical and constructive inquiry in the search for a unified and comprehensive basis in the incarnate grace of God for all theology. (1990, 1-2)

It would seem to be the case that we must place Barth not only in the company of Schleiermacher, Calvin, and Luther, but also in that of Augustine and Athanasius. He was a truly great theologian.

Crossing the Atlantic Ocean, we note that Reinhold Niebuhr (1892-1971) was probably the most attractive and influential exponent of neo-orthodoxy in America. He began his ministry in 1915 in Detroit, committed to liberal theology, and pastored there until 1928. While in the Detroit pastorate, he recognized man's absolute need for the grace of God, as well as his need to turn to a modern form of orthodoxy, which owed much to Barth and Brunner. This can be read in his *An Interpretation of*

Christian Ethics (1937) and his massive *The Nature and Destiny of Man* (1949). It may be claimed that his neo-orthodoxy rested on two pillars, both of which were indispensable to his theology. One is the utter powerlessness of the world to save and to redeem itself. The other is that the Gospel of God, concerning Jesus Christ, tells the truth about the world and also supplies the grace of God wherein is salvation and redemption.

Reinhold's brother, H. Richard Niebuhr (1894-1962), a professor at Yale, was also critical of liberalism and sympathetic to Barth's theology. In his *Kingdom of God in America* (1937) he had some sharp comments to offer. Liberal theology "established continuity between God and man by adjusting God to man" (192). And "a God without wrath brought men without sin into a kingdom without judgment through the ministrations of a Christ without a cross" (193). His book *The Meaning of Revelation* (1940, 1962) is seen by many as a major theological basis of what is now called narrative theology (to which we shall return in chapter six).

Over in Scotland there were also two brilliant brothers who had been attracted away from liberalism toward dialectical theology and neo-orthodoxy—John Baillie (1886-1960) and Donald Baillie (1887-1954). Their books reflect the British compromise position, which sought to have the best of all worlds but leaned toward Brunner and Barth. Donald's *God Was in Christ* (originally published in 1948 and often reprinted) was one of the textbooks that I had to read in King's College, University of London in 1962 in my study of Christian doctrine.

From the writings of Barth and those of his followers in Europe and North America it is possible to summarize neo-orthodoxy in terms of five specific emphases. First, in contrast to liberal theology, neo-orthodoxy appeared to have a high view of the divine inspiration, unity, and authority of the Bible. The Scriptures contain, it was affirmed, not correct human thoughts about God but God's thoughts concerning man. The holy books set forth not lessons on how we should talk to God, but details of what God Himself says to us. The Bible declares not what we are to do to have a right relationship with God, but what He has done to place us in a right relationship with Himself. Furthermore, while the general findings of higher criticism were accepted (e.g., that Moses is not the author of the Pentateuch, but rather that the first five books of the Old Testament are composed from various literary sources; that Mark is the earliest gospel, and both Matthew and Mark are dependent on it; and that Paul is not the author of the Epistle to the Hebrews), it was nevertheless claimed that there is a supernatural character to the Bible, and this makes it entirely different in religious value to all other books. This is because it witnesses to Jesus Christ, the living Word of God.

Second, the neo-orthodox insisted that the revelation from God on which Christianity is based is unique. There is no continuity between other religions and Christianity or between natural religion and Christianity. Barth gave his famous *nein* to the possibility of a natural theology based on the observation of the cosmos and the human race. Brunner severely criticized him for this in 1934, and while Barth modified his position as the years went by, he never changed it fundamentally. His followers, however, tended to move toward Calvin and Brunner, both of whom allowed for the general revelation of God in nature and thus, in principle, the possibility of a natural theology.

Third, the neo-orthodox emphasized that Jesus, the Christ, was truly God in the flesh. Jesus was not merely the fullest spiritual and moral development of man, but He was in the words of the Nicene Creed "very God of very God, one in substance with the Father." Thus, He was one person with two natures, and in His human nature He truly suffered and died as a sacrifice for the sins of the world. Yet God, the Father, by the Holy Spirit, raised Him from the dead; and this resurrection was nothing less than a mighty act of God and the establishment of the new creation, the new order of the kingdom of God. In fact, the whole New Testament was written in the light of the resurrection of Jesus from the dead, and this message was the central proclamation of the early church.

Fourth, the neo-orthodox were very much aware of the inherent sinfulness of man and insisted that it is because of its sinfulness that the human race needs the grace of God and the gift of eternal salvation. They spoke freely of the limitations and corruption of human nature and followed the Danish thinker Søren Kierkegaard in their descriptions of the weakness of man before God, who is infinitely and qualitatively different to man. Aspects of this approach are found in the book *The Nature and Destiny of Man* by Reinhold Niebuhr, who makes clear that the sin of pride is so pervasive that it affects all interpersonal relationships.

Finally, neo-orthodoxy is characterized by the constant contrast between God and man, eternity and time, heaven and earth, grace and sin. God is holy and the wholly other, for nothing can be compared to Him. His majesty is in total contrast to both the sinfulness and the greatness of man. God is certainly immanent and present within the created order, but His immanence flows from, and is dependent on, His glorious transcendence because of the infinite, qualitative difference between the living God (the Father, the Son, and the Holy Spirit) and the human creature made in His image and likeness.

Neo-orthodoxy was the dominant theology in American old-line Protestantism (with the exception of the Episcopal Church, which was influenced by British theology) from the 1930s to the 1960s. Since then it has maintained a steady following but is now only minimally influential within the old-line denominations. Yet, when it arrived on the scene between the First and Second World Wars, it gained great attention and a wide following in North America. In 1933 John C. Bennett claimed that "the most important fact about contemporary American theology is the disintegration of Liberalism" (cited by Henry, *Fifty Years*, 62). About the same time, C. S. Patten commented that before Barth's influence was felt, the old liberal theology patterned after Ritschl's teaching reigned without serious rivals in academia. Therefore, such doctrines as "the Trinity, Incarnation, Miracles, the Fall of man, the Atonement, and Heaven and Hell, dropped out of discussion" (ibid., 68).

In 1961 Harry Emerson Fosdick, then in his eighties, was interviewed by a Canadian reporter, Kenneth Bagnell. Reporting that interview in the Toronto *Globe and Mail*, October 8, 1969, after the death of Fosdick, Bagnell wrote:

> When we talked of changing theological fashions, he was more restrained, insisting that he was an old man and had not kept up. "But I will say that no theological emphasis has a hold on permanency. I was in a discussion at Union Seminary [New York] some years ago and a professor said that liberalism was through and Barthianism and Neo-Orthodoxy were in. So I said I'd like to stay around long enough to see what followed." And so he did. For the sixties have been hard on Neo-Orthodoxy.

But, we reflect, the sixties were hard on most types of orthodoxies and traditionalisms.

ADAM AND EVE'S GRANDCHILDREN

To return to the period 1930 to 1960, we may observe that it seemed that neo-orthodoxy, which eclipsed evangelicalism in the academic (but not popular) arena, had crushed liberal theology by 1960. But this sentence of death was premature. Certainly the specific forms of liberal theology expressed in Harnack's *What Is Christianity?* (1901) and preached by Harry Emerson Fosdick in New York City in the 1930s were gone forever. However, the family of liberal theology lived on not only in the theology of correlation from Paul Tillich and process theology/panentheism from Charles Hartshorne (to which we turn in chapter four) but also in scattered attempts to revive the best of classic liberalism in the old-line churches.

Further, the former liberal theology multiplied in its grandchildren who, as we shall see, bear such varied names as the theology of hope, theology of play, liturgical theology, liberation theology, feminist theology, third-world theology, black theology, hermeneutical theology, political theology, and revisionist theology. These grandchildren may readily be encountered within the deliberations and reports of the World Council of Churches as well as in many seminaries, conventions, synods, and publications of Protestant and Roman Catholic churches from the late 1960s through to the 1990s.

However, of the old, classic, liberal Protestantism (which is still embraced here and there in America in a modern form by some of the older generation—e.g., the sociologist, Peter Berger, whom we will meet in chapter three), it has been said that it is like the Smithsonian dinosaur whose structural skeleton remains but whose heart has stopped beating. Only time will tell whether there will be a revival of classic liberalism. Right now it appears that its grandchildren are very much present in the central offices of the old-line denominations.

Moreover, where churches use written forms for worship, the grandchildren can also be found alive and well, explicitly or implicitly present, in the newer liturgies or forms of worship. Here they express themselves via the adoption of inclusive language for God and man, the adoption of novel doctrines of sin and salvation, the adoption of modern causes as the essence or purpose of Christianity, and the adoption of an emphasis on the affirming and empowering of individuals in the local church—a community of faith (in contrast to the biblical household of faith).

Our task in this book is primarily to seek to understand and explain those whom we may deem to be the grandchildren of original liberal theology or the great grandchildren of the first parents (the intellectual outlook and the religious feeling of the early nineteenth century). These twentieth-century offspring have obviously intermarried with other families (e.g., those of Eastern religions and of modern psychologies and philosophies) to produce more descendants whom we may deem to be (in the spirit of the age) not male or female but androgynous. Thus, in modern pluralist, multicultural, and democratic America you can find many different descendants of the first parents not only within academic institutions—departments of religion and theology of the universities and colleges and seminaries—but also in the headquarters of the old-line denominations and in many suburban churches.

Further, and this is very important, these grandchildren have also intermarried with post-Vatican II Roman Catholic families. In any survey of the post-1960s revisionist theologies as well as liberation, feminist, and environmentalist theologies, it is impossible fully to prize the Protestant and Roman Catholic apart from the other, for they are in a sense symbiotic. Already we noted in chapter one how modern liturgies in both the Roman and Protestant churches are very similar in structure and content. Here we can add that modern forms of theology in both Catholicism and Protestantism are also very similar. Since this is so, it is both necessary and helpful, I think, to add to this chapter an appendix, briefly explaining the profound change in theology in Roman Catholicism over the last forty or fifty years.

We must not forget, of course, that there are other different families of theology present within Christendom today. Their parentage goes back through many centuries. The one that is apparently attracting the greatest attention in America today, because it is least touched by modernity, is that which is found within Orthodoxy and that comes from the Greek fathers of the early church—Athanasius, Basil, and Chrysostom, for example. It is experienced liturgically in the ancient liturgies of St. Basil and St. Chrysostom in the Greek, Russian, and Antiochene Orthodox churches. Running a close second is that which is associated with the Latin fathers, Augustine and Gregory the Great, and their medieval successors, Anselm and Aquinas. This, too, can be experienced liturgically through attendance at the (pre-Vatican II, Roman or Tridentine Rite) Latin Mass that is proving increasingly popular (much to the embarrassment of the large liberal element in modern Roman Catholicism) in both Canada and the United States. In fact, all the signs are that traditional patristic and medieval theology of both Greek and

Latin origins is making a small but sustained resurgence in Western Christianity today.

Likewise, among traditional Protestants, the families of theology that began in the sixteenth and seventeenth centuries in old Europe still are to be found, though the search for and commitment to them is not as widespread or profound as that for the older Latin and Greek theologies. Although these Lutheran, Reformed, and Anglican theologies reveal among themselves many differences in method and in content, they have also much in common. For example, they all have a very high estimate of the Holy Scriptures as the Word of God written. They use, where necessary, the higher criticism with care and reserve, and they all receive the classical dogmas of the Holy Trinity and of Christology as found in the Nicene Creed (381) and in the definition of the person of Christ from the Council of Chalcedon (451). These doctrines are embodied in the confessional documents and/or liturgies of these churches, which also contain, of course, the emphasis on justification by faith through the grace of God.

Regrettably modern Lutheran, Reformed or Presbyterian, and Anglican churches seem to pay little attention to their traditional confessions and liturgies. They have been deeply affected by liberal theology and its offspring. Thus, the traditional theology from the period of the Reformation is to be found in small pockets here and there in the old denominations and, more self-consciously perhaps, in offshoots from them (e.g., the newer continuing Presbyterian and Anglican denominations, as well as in the Missouri and Wisconsin Synods of Lutheranism).

Now, it would be foolish to assume that these ancient families have entered and lived through the nineteenth and twentieth centuries without being affected by the *Zeitgeist* of these times. They have been tempted to ignore modernity, enter into themselves, and become seemingly irrelevant to modern life and needs. They have also been tempted to accommodate their doctrine to the drift of modern philosophies and psychologies in order to be seen as relevant. There have been injuries, casualties, and defections, but the traditional families remain inside and outside the old-line or mainline denominations still bearing their original names and family likeness.

Since many evangelicals do not trace their origins back to the Reformation but to nineteenth- or twentieth-century roots, questions arise: Where do we place the evangelical and fundamentalist theologies of the last fifty years? From which families do they descend? Are they a kind of marriage between one or another of the classic forms of Protestant theology and aspects of the spirit of the modern age? To what extent have they absorbed the central themes of Romanticism (e.g., meeting God in the feelings through expressive individualism) and produced subjectivist theology? Certainly all of them claim to be biblical; but this claim, in and of itself, may mean no more than that they make much use of the Bible, quoting it or referring to it frequently. For example, do they treat the Bible as if it were a great container of inspired, God-breathed statements (i.e., verses) from which one takes such texts as are appropriate or helpful at any one time? Or is the Bible like a constitutional document, which is supremely authoritative but is used and interpreted to meet modern changing contexts and conditions? Or is the Bible approached through what may be called a viewing grid, so that the Bible (through proof-texts) serves to confirm the grid (e.g., one or another form of dispensationalism)? Such is the variety of forms of fundamentalism and popular evangelicalism that simple answers to their relation to historic Protestantism and the culture of modernity are not available (but see further the epilogue to this book).

FOR FURTHER READING

Berkhof, Hendrikus. *Two Hundred Years of Theology*. Grand Rapids, Mich.: Eerdmans, 1989.

Hunter, James D. *American Evangelicalism: Conservative*

Religion and the Quandary of Modernity. New Brunswick, N.J.: Rutgers University Press, 1983.

Henry, Carl F. H. *Fifty Years of Protestant Theology.* Boston: Wilde, 1950.

Heron, Alasdair I. C. *A Century of Protestant Theology.* Philadelphia: Westminster, 1980.

Hutchison, William R. *The Modernist Impulse in American Protestantism.* New York: Oxford University Press, 1982.

Mackintosh, Hugh Ross. *Types of Modern Theology: Schleiermacher to Barth.* London: Nisbet, 1937.

Reardon, Bernard M. G. *Liberal Protestantism.* London: Adam and Charles Black, 1968.

Smart, Ninian, et al. *Nineteenth Century Religious Thought in the West.* 3 vols. New York: Cambridge University Press, 1985.

Thielicke, Helmut. *Modern Faith and Thought.* Grand Rapids, Mich.: Eerdmans, 1990.

Van Dusen, Henry P. *The Vindication of Liberal Theology.* New York: Scribners, 1963.

Wells, David F. *No Place for Truth: Or, Whatever happened to Evangelical Theology?* Grand Rapids, Mich.: Eerdmans, 1993.

APPENDIX: ROMAN CATHOLIC THEOLOGY

The Roman Catholic Church in Europe and America existed in the same general culture as the Protestant churches. Unlike the Protestants, however, the Roman Church had a powerful central organization in terms of the papacy and the Vatican City. Faced with the questions and pressures that caused Protestants to adopt liberal theology, Roman Catholic seminaries and bishops were directed to look back and find their theology in that of the great medieval theologian and philosopher Thomas Aquinas (1225-74) and in his major interpreters of the Counter-Reformation of the sixteenth and seventeenth centuries. By his encyclical of 1879, *Aeterni Patris*, Pope Leo XIII launched a massive revival of Thomist or Scholastic method in philosophy and theology.

While it is true that the Scholastic way of doing theology and its relation with philosophy was new (modern) in medieval Scholasticism, for it was part of an emerging civilization in Europe, the neo-Scholasticism of Pope Leo XIII was self-consciously anti-modern in the late nineteenth century. It was a determined attempt to look away from modernity into medieval antiquity in order to maintain and control dogma, doctrine, and morality in a fast-changing world. With only a few exceptions, this neo-Scholastic approach and method dominated Catholic intellectual life until the Second Vatican Council that opened in 1962.

The Scholastic method emphasized logical relations and metaphysical distinctions among the various truths to which biblical and patristic sources witnessed. In the *Summa Theologiae* of Thomas Aquinas, this method is used with great power and clarity. With the help of Aristotelian philosophy he gave to the inherited Augustinian theology from the late patristic era a thoroughly rational basis. He carefully distinguished between a double order of knowledge and being (a natural basis and a supernatural superstructure), two powers of knowledge (natural reason and faith through grace), two levels of knowledge (natural truth and revealed truth through grace), and two sciences (philosophy and theology). It was this great work that was a primary textbook for the learning of doctrine.

It was accompanied by another text, this time a nineteenth-century compilation. Affectionately (or, these days, pejoratively) known as "Denzinger," it was a collection of the statements of Scripture, the Fathers, and the Councils on all aspects of doctrine. Its full title was, *A Manual of the Church's Doctrinal Decisions*, with a first edition in 1854, the Marian year (i.e., when the dogma of the Immaculate Conception was promulgated). Since 1854 it has gone through many editions.

Virtually no place was given in either text to the historical situationalism of these truths (i.e., when and where they were first stated and how the context affected the way they were stated). Thus, Roman Catholic seminaries, unlike Protestant academies, had little, if any, of the use of the historical-critical method in either the study of the Bible or of the Fathers. Those who made use of this method were known as the Catholic modernists. Hans Küng, the Tübingen theologian, was trained in this atmosphere, and, writing in the mid-1980s after he had shaken himself free of it, he complained of the Vatican bureaucracy that tried "to impose the medieval-Counter-Reformation paradigm on the whole church in the grand style (Neo-Scholasticism, Neo-Romanticism, Neo-Gothic art and architecture, Neo-Gregorianism)" (*Theology for the Third Millennium*, 1988, 185).

The first major challenge to the reign of neo-Scholastic theology occurred in France after the Second World War and is associated with Yves Congar, Henri du Lubac, Jean Daniélou, and Henri Bouillard. Through their writings the modernity of science and history began to make an impact not only on theology but also on liturgy. Then there appeared on the scene two Jesuits—the French Canadian Bernard Lonergan and the German Karl Rahner, in whose work a serious challenge to the old neo-Scholasticism began. It is common to follow Otto Muck's argument in his study of them in *The Transcendental Method* (1968) and portray both Rahner and Lonergan as developing a revision of traditional Thomism in terms of the transcendental method known as transcendental Thomism. This method is an attempt to uncover, at the preconceptual level in human beings, a universal experience of divine presence or grace.

Since the Vatican Council in the mid-1960s, it is fair to claim that both Rahner and Lonergan have been deeply influential in the speedy attempt by Roman Catholic universities and seminaries to make their theology truly contemporary. The Vatican Council opened the windows of the Church to the world, and in the powerful winds of modernity that blew through the church the moderately-revisionist theology of Rahner and Lonergan seemed sure anchors on which to hold. However, Hans Küng, who shared for a long time an enthusiasm for the new insights and fresh air that Rahner's writings generated, now stated:

> For a long time, schooled as I was by Aristotle, Thomas, Hegel and Heidegger, I have admired Rahner's lofty dialectic, just as I have affirmed (and still do affirm) a concern for the unity and continuity of the church expressed so diversely in this interpretation of creeds and doctrinal propositions. Isn't this [Rahner's theology, which emphasized historical and temporal relativity] a brilliantly successful way to interpret a formula "dialectically" so that the language remains (and that is the main thing for "conservatives"), but the content is remolded (which is what the "progressives" are interested in)? (*Theology for the Third Millennium*, 187)

In fact, Küng believes that Rahner was the last great (and stimulating) neo-Scholastic.

Maybe Rahner was the last great neo-Scholastic, but he was also deeply influenced by Martin Heidegger, the German existentialist philosopher. In his book *Being and Time*, Heidegger argued that the ontological categories used from the period of Greek philosophy (Plato) through to the seventeenth century (Descartes) are inadequate and unable to describe the reality of the temporarility, historicity, and facticity of human existence and life in the world. Therefore, he replaced the old categories with new ones that he called existentials. The new categories characterize what is specific to human existence in the world: being toward death, care, self-interpretation. Rahner accepted and used Heidegger's new categories. Moreover, Lonergan, in a parallel manner, dropped the traditional faculty psychology of Scholasticism and moved to what is called intentionality analysis. The result of this was that the basic terms and relations of systematic theology became for him psychological rather than metaphysical as in the older theology.

Certainly, in the writings of such theologians as Hans Küng himself, along with the American David Tracy and the Dutchman Edward Schillebeeckx, modern Roman Catholic theology has moved on from Lonergan and Rahner into what can best be termed an ecumenical theology from a Roman Catholic perspective (see further the appendix to chapter five). Further, in the freedom of post-Vatican II, there have appeared a continuous stream of modern theologies of liberation, feminism, environmentalism, and spirituality. These often also have an ecumenical face to them. Thus, while the forces of modernity were gradually accommodated or absorbed by the major Protestant churches over a period of a century or so, the Roman Catholic Church has had to accommodate and absorb these forces in the space of only twenty or thirty years. Visibly this is symbolized in much modern Roman Catholic worship where the emphasis is more on the experience of community (celebration) than on the majesty and transcendence of God (reverence).

A very readable and illuminating introduction to modern Roman Catholic theology in America is provided by *Systematic Theology: Roman Catholic Perspectives* (2 vols., 1991). Significantly, in this ecumenical age it was published by the Lutheran Augsburg Press. It is a collaborative work, and in their carefully written preface the editors, Francis Schüssler Fiorenza and John P. Galvin, tell us that they had five specific goals in mind that they shared with their contributors.

The first was that the work was to be rooted in Roman Catholic theology. Of course, they did not mean the old deductive method of the traditional manuals of theology. Rather, they meant that they were to present the teaching of the Roman Church and discuss significant theological reflection from leading Catholic theologians (e.g., by Karl Rahner, Edward Schillebeeckx, Yves Congar, Henri de Lubac, Hans Urs von Balthasar, Joseph Ratzinger, and Gustavo Gutierrez) since Vatican II.

The second goal was that the work was to reveal what a major impetus had come to Roman Catholic theology from historical studies. Not only has there been the adoption of the historical-critical study of the Scriptures, but there has been a utilization of the historical method for the examination of the whole tradition of the Western church. This has led to changed attitudes toward, and new interpretations of, the tradition.

The third goal was that the work should take into account current hermeneutical theories and philosophical reflections. It is the case that philosophers such as Kant and Heidegger, as well as Gadamer and Ricoeur, have deeply affected contemporary theologians. "Phenomenology as well as critical theory, literary theory as well as neopragmatism, have all had their impact."

The fourth goal was that the work should take into account the ecumenical dimension of modern theology, especially the consensus reached by various interdenominational theological commissions. This meant that the contributors "were to explain Roman Catholic theological statements in a way that is sensitive to other Christian churches, especially where the views of other Christians should lead Roman Catholic theologians to be more self-critical."

Finally, the fifth goal was that the work should be attentive to the current emphasis on practice, which has been especially evident in recent theologies of liberation. "Roman Catholics and all Christians should be sensitive to the social and practical dimensions of their beliefs and reflections."

Thus, in presenting a post-Vatican II, modern Roman Catholic theology, influenced by historical and ecumenical studies, open to new philosophical currents, and sensitive to diverse historical and cultural situations, the Roman Catholic writers have provided a text that could also be used (and is being used) in a modern Protestant seminary.

Chapter 3

Environment: The Context of Modern Theology

The grandchildren (e.g., existential, hermeneutical, political, liberation, and feminist theologies) of their distinguished nineteenth-century forebears may be said to make two basic claims. They are what they are not only because of their heredity but also because of their environment. In fact, their heredity and environment are seemingly inextricably intertwined. In the last chapter we noticed their heredity via liberal theology, and inevitably this involved some comment on their environment.

Here we must reflect primarily on their environment in a post-World War II and post-colonial era. First of all, however, in order to get as broad a context as possible, it will be appropriate to notice the environmental factors that affected this family in its origins before 1800, as well as in both the nineteenth and twentieth centuries.

NEW WORLDS WITHOUT AND WITHIN

One must take into account at least five areas of the development of human knowledge in order to appreciate why the modern worldview is different from that of earlier centuries. Much has been written on these themes; thus they will be presented only in summary form here.

In the first place, it can be claimed that due to the work of

Bacon, Harvey, Kepler, Galileo, Huygens, and Newton (not to mention Descartes, Pascal, Locke, Spinoza, and Leibniz) in the seventeenth century, modern man has a different view of the cosmos than did the Reformers Luther and Calvin and such earlier giants as Thomas Aquinas and Augustine of Hippo. For us, the earth is not perceived as the center of the universe; we have the idea of a vast universe of which the earth is merely a very minute part. This knowledge has not only caused theologians to reevaluate the cosmology of the Bible and the way the church has understood how God acts as Creator and Sustainer; it has also raised questions as to the nature of the supernatural, the identity and place of heaven and hell, and whether the Son of God was incarnate in other worlds as well as this one.

In the second place, it can be asserted that, due to the writings of modern philosophers (Descartes, Locke, Hume, and Kant, for example) of the seventeenth and eighteenth centuries, modern man has a different view of his identity and place in the universe than did Protestants and Catholics of the sixteenth century and before. Not only has he had to come to terms with the new physics, astronomy, and cosmology, but he has also had to learn to understand himself in a different light. He is now seen as an embodied, autonomous self who thinks of himself as an individual alongside other individuals and defines his individuality in terms of both his inner feelings and his outer job/work. Previously he was an immortal soul (an embodied soul), a person in relation to other persons and in relation to God, in whose image he is made and from whom he received a vocation and purpose in life. He is now an individual who receives and interprets his sense experience of this world, recognizing that he can have no specific, direct experience and knowledge of God. Previously he was a person, a living soul, through whose spirit he was in relation to God, the Father, in Christ and through the Holy Spirit, as well as in relation to others in the communion of the saints. In addition, through God's self-revelation he had access to real knowledge of God as the Father of the Lord Jesus Christ.

In the third place, it can be argued that the impact of the theory of evolution was a greater shock to the European Christian mind than was the arrival of the new physics and cosmology. At least the latter left man as the highest of the creatures, the one who had the ability to think about the cosmos in a rational way. But the impact of the theory of the evolution of the species, which we particularly associate with the name of Charles Darwin (1809-82), was to place man alongside other living creatures as the highest of a kind, rather than as a unique phenomenon. In terms of theology, the theory raised profound questions concerning the mode and nature of the activity of God in the universe as its Creator and Sustainer and concerning the interpretation of such biblical passages as Genesis 1–3.

In the fourth place, it can be shown that the establishment of the strange new world within human beings by depth-psychology, begun by Sigmund Freud (1856-1939), has virtually revolutionized the way modern people understand human personality, experience, and consciousness. In particular, it was Freud who discovered the vital role of unconscious motivations and opened them up to study and to therapy. Then it was Carl Gustav Jung (1875-1961) who pointed not only to the personal conscious and unconscious factors in the human psyche but also to a second psychic system of a collective, universal, and impersonal nature. This collective unconscious, claimed Jung, is inherited by all, and its contents he called archetypes. The principles of depth psychology do not eliminate religion; however, they do raise serious questions about the traditional doctrine of man as made in the image of God, as fallen from that image, as inheriting original sin, and as living as a sinner before God. Thus, it is not surprising that some theologians feel the need to develop and adapt the received doctrine of man as sinner in the light of modern psychology. Such developments naturally affect preaching, teaching, counseling, spiritual direction, views of sanctification and deification, and contents of liturgies (e.g., the confession of sin).

Finally, in the fifth place, it hardly needs to be stated that the arrival and development of what is called the science of biblical criticism (the historical-critical method) has profoundly affected not only the way people read the Bible but also the use of the Bible by theologians. What for the seventeenth century was a collection of holy books in one Book—an authoritative collection of authoritative books written by men but inspired and guaranteed by God—has become for moderns a Jewish and Christian collection of books that were written by men who described primarily the religious experience of men in various places and different times. Thus, the Scriptures are open to the charges, made by advocates of modern political correctness, of patriarchalism, sexism, and androcentricism. In general, modern Christians accept that the collection is unique, containing priceless wisdom and spiritual knowledge; they also accept that in reading and commenting on this Holy Book over the centuries the church has also bequeathed to us great treasures of moral and spiritual truth; yet what they cannot accept is that the Bible is actually the written Word of God, that it is the Word of God in the words of man. What is emphasized today is the human character of Scripture and the absolute need to interpret it in terms of the original situation in and for which it was written. Having ascertained this, the theologian then has to ask what meaning that original message has for people today in a totally different culture and civilization.

It is easy to forget, and needs to be recalled, that these cultural and mental revolutions took place in a rapidly changing social scene. Through the effects of industrialization, public health, and the impact and availability of technology, people changed their thinking—their expectations. In fact, where people lived, how they traveled, how they dressed, what they ate, how they spent their time, and how they faced illness, disease, and death all underwent changes. A changing mind-set accompanied a changing environment, and a changing environment had its part in changing the mind-set. What would Luther and Calvin make of a modern hospital, a fax machine, travel in a jumbo jet, and pictures of the universe taken by cameras in outer space?

THE FACT AND CONSCIOUSNESS OF CHOICE

Of all the writers who describe and analyze modernity, perhaps the most readable and illuminating is Peter Berger. We turn to his *Heretical Imperative* (1979) for insight into the reality of choice as a modern phenomenon. The Western world is like a massive supermarket, containing a vast array of possible ways of believing, behaving, thinking, and acting.

Berger points out that modern consciousness arises in the movement from fate to choice. In traditional society, much of what a person is and does is governed by custom and culture. There is little or no choice in what one wears, how one relates to others, whom one marries, where one lives, how one behaves, and where one goes. People in such societies do not generally believe they are missing anything in being governed by fate because their consciousness is formed by the presuppositions and ethos of their traditions.

In contrast, people in modernity (be they in Western nations or the big cities of the Third World) not only have to make choices all the time, but their consciousness is formed by this reality of choice. For example, what to wear, where to live, what to eat, and where to work are choices because Western life seems like one big superstore where all varieties and sizes of goods are available for purchase. In particular, the arrival of birth-control methods has revolutionized the approach to parenthood and the exercise of sexuality. Moreover, the pluralism generated by modern society has brought new phrases into ordinary language. Westerners speak of a sexual preference, meaning the choice to be heterosexual or homosexual (or both), in a culture that makes all options possible; they also speak of a religious preference, meaning the choice to practice this or that faith in a society where there is a great variety of religious practices and observances, especially in big cities or metropolitan areas.

What may be claimed to be unique in a religious sense in the modern situation is the obvious availability not only of a vast number of Christian churches, societies, and denominations but also, often in an attractive form, the presence of sects, cults, and Eastern religions. In a large bookstore in a university city it is possible to spend several hundred dollars and get in good translation the classics of all the world religions and thus, potentially at least, to become familiar with them all. Usually there will be classes at local colleges to help in this process of knowing about the variety and content of religions. The general effect of all this on the thinking person is to make religious uncertainty or religious eclecticism more probable than religious certainty and unshakable convictions. In such a context, clear convictions on religion are then viewed as odd or undesirable, and pluralism and relativism are taken for granted. Religious preference is thus the necessary partner of choice.

In other words, modernity multiplies choices and at the same time reduces the scope of what is experienced as destiny. It is not only that the modern person has the opportunity to make choices but that he also lives in the necessity of making choices. Whereas in the premodern world people simply accepted religious tradition, submitting to it as they did to floods, earthquakes, and fires, now in the modern world people are forced to choose their worldview and philosophy of life.

Along with this consciousness of choice there is a strong accentuation of the subjective side of human existence. Not able to find in pluralistic society one clear answer to any possible question, and living in the reality of relativism, a person is driven to look within himself—to find his own self and get in touch with his feelings. He looks for certainties within himself because they do not exist in his external situation. Hence, we have seen in Western society in recent decades (in the modern novel, play, art, psychologies, and psychotherapies, not to mention advertising, soap operas, and talk shows) an ever-increasing attention to human subjectivity. Obviously this is because it is widely believed and felt that the socially defined universe cannot be relied on any longer. Consequently, in the process the external world becomes more questionable and the inner world becomes more complex.

It is not difficult, then, to understand what Sartre's phrase "condemned to freedom" can mean in modernity where a person can experience liberation and alienation simultaneously. A sense of alienation may bring nostalgia for a restored world of order, solidarity, and meaning, while a sense of freedom may bring a desire to shed all constraints and rules and be oneself. Agreeing with Berger, John K. Simmons comments:

> We should never forget that although modernity has compelled us to choose from a multitude of institutional and cognitive possibilities, it is never an easy project. It is not simply a matter of pushing the shopping cart down the aisles of Weltanschauung's Supermart snatching a sack of Mystical Munchies, grabbing a bag of Yin-Yang Flakes, a package of Buddha-Biscuits, a can of Desert Fathers' Soup Mix. Always there remains an unsatisfied hunger for authority. It is not enough to choose. A person needs to feel that the choice is right. The paradigms present in the chosen worldview need to describe accurately in-world experience. (1986, 171)

Simmons then joins Berger in claiming that if the modern, pluralistic situation is taken seriously, there are only really three basic options for religious thought (or three types of theology possible) today.

Berger calls these options the deductive, the reductive, and the inductive and uses three famous Christian theologians (Barth, Bultmann, and Schleiermacher) to illustrate the three types. We shall return to the details of this typology in chapter five. Here we need only note that, facing this modern situation of being condemned to freedom and of getting in touch with feelings, modern theology is seemingly forced to take serious account of modern experience (not only in general terms of the world but also in specific terms of the individualized, autonomous self). Accordingly, in differing ways, and not unexpectedly, both conservative theologies (e.g., charismatic, evangelical, and pietist) and liberation theologies (e.g., feminist, Third World, and black) are deeply experiential in their character and claims.

Berger himself favors the inductive method, which makes sense in the light of the reality of modernity. It is to turn, on the one hand, to personal experience of God and the universe and, on the other, to the religious experience based on a particular tradition or traditions (e.g., Lutheranism and a particular form of church music) as the ground of all religious affirmations. Here traditions are understood as bodies of evidence concerning religious experience and the insights deriving from experience. The greatest ever exponent of this type of theology was, of course, Friedrich Schleiermacher, a thinker whom Berger much admires. In this approach, the committed Christian has to be clear that open-mindedness does not lead into open-endedness and that proclamation of the Gospel does not become merely the offering of a hypothesis about an option within modern life!

A NEW MIDDLE CLASS

With Berger's help we also need to notice and incorporate into our thinking one further dimension of sociological analysis of the modern world, especially as it is experienced in America. This will help us understand why it is that the large Protestant denominations, and more recently the Roman Catholic Church, have since the 1960s seemingly embraced theologies of modernity with relatively little pain and often with celebratory zeal. Berger's description of the bifurcation of the middle class since the Second World War illuminates the question as to why the grandchildren of liberal theology have moved with comparative ease from the seminaries and universities into the pulpits, pews, and politics of American churches in recent decades.

In his essay "Different Gospels: The Social Sources of Apostasy," originally delivered as the Erasmus Lecture in January 1987 in New York City, Berger notes first of all that culture Protestantism was alive and well in the 1950s. What we call the old-line or mainline denominations existed in a generally happy symbiosis with middle-class culture. There was little tension between Episcopalians, Methodists, Presbyterians, Lutherans, and Baptists and their cultural milieu. America was O.K., and the middle-class way of life was O.K. God seemed to approve and bless both. Further, as Daniel Day Williams made clear in his book *What Present-day Theologians Are Thinking* (1952), all seemed well in the theological world. Theology was also alive and well.

This happy situation could not last, and one of the major social factors to disturb it was the bifurcation of the middle class (as explained by the new-class thesis held by thinkers of the right and left of the political spectrum). The causes of this bifurcation are primarily technological and economic and relate to the obvious fact that in an advanced industrial society fewer people are needed in the labor force to provide the necessary material production. So a growing number of people are released and enter into what may be called miscellaneous services (the "quaternary" sector). Within this sector there is what may be called the knowledge industry. This is devoted to the production and distribution of symbolic knowledge, and those who are involved in this by way of making their living from it are called the "new class." Examples are the people involved in communication (e.g., via the media, public relations, lobbying in Washington), in education (of all kinds and for all ages and groups), in therapy (for children and adults with a panorama of presenting problems), in the bureaucracies (particularly but not solely associated with federal and state governments) and, for our purposes very importantly, in religion (both as pastors and as religious bureaucrats).

This new class was and is a minority. However, since it operates in key institutions and provides the symbols and images by which modern society, in general, perceives and understands itself, its influence is out of proportion to its numbers. The political stance of this knowledge industry is usually to the left of center. One possible reason for this is that the new class stands to gain by a greater role of government in modern life, especially the expansion of the provisions of the welfare state. Another is that the knowledge industry has an ever-growing role if it can appeal to a limitless number of human rights—that is, if it can persuade us all that each of us is an individual with a seemingly limitless possibility for discovering within us a yet-unproclaimed human right.

In contrast, the old middle class, situated to the right of center in political activity, was, and remains, the class of the business community and the traditional professions.

If we relate this to the situation in the old-line denominations since the late 1960s when they began to experience a large loss of members, we notice that the old middle class has been slowly but surely replaced by the new class in the clerical and lay leadership, so that the latter now represent a majority. This explains why the political agenda of the new class (suitably adorned with "God-language") has been widely adopted within the mainline churches. Much the same process has occurred within the Roman Catholic Church and Judaism over the last thirty or so years. Hence, it is often the case that the most outspoken people for so-called left-wing political causes, or for socialist agendas at home and abroad, or for new definitions of what is a family and what is marriage, are the senior clergy of these denominations. They know that the majority of the elected representatives of their churches support them in such declarations. Conservative evangelicals have tended to refer to the new philosophy and agenda of the liberal churches as secular humanism and have produced a stream of books on the topic since the 1980s.

It seems to me that this analysis of the emergence of the new class helps to explain several important events in the life of the mainline Protestant denominations as well as of Roman Catholicism. First, it explains the growing phenomenon of community churches, those independent, interdenominational congregations to which thousands of laity who dislike the new ways and speech have quietly moved. Second, it explains the culture wars that rage from time to time in and around the churches, explained—at least in part—in terms of the clash of values of the old middle class and the new class. In these wars the traditional working-class and blue-collar-class church members stand very much with the old middle class because they share values. In general, opposition to the new morality (i.e., to such things as situation ethics and the moves to bless homosexual unions), to the new forms of worship (e.g., the new inclusive language lectionaries and liturgies within the Episcopal and Lutheran churches), and new theology (e.g., that which denies original sin and emphasizes that the local congregation is the community of celebration, where individuals are affirmed and accepted) comes from members of the old middle class or the working class.

In other words, without the emergence of the new class it is difficult to see how the modern grandchildren (e.g., feminist theology) of those faraway nineteenth-century parents could either be born or thrive in American society. Likewise, without the continuance of the church-going members of the old middle class and of the working class, it is difficult to see how there could be either visible opposition to the new theologies or meaningful support for the traditional theologies of the old-line Protestants as well as the old traditions of the Roman Catholic and Greek/Russian Orthodox churches.

What appears to be the case now, in both Protestant denominations and in Roman Catholicism, is that instead of there being a happy and symbiotic union of the old middle class and pre-1960s culture, there is a symbiotic bond between the new middle class with the post-1960s culture. In this modern culture the fact of the common vote is equated with common insight, and a common access to truth is confused with a common possession of truth. So the pollsters tell us what the people feel and desire, and this becomes the truth for that generation. Obviously in this new relationship, evident in the old-line denominations, we notice that the description of the identity and role of the clergyperson has necessarily changed. She or he is now perceived as a religious professional, whose primary models are those of the manager and the psychologist. Their role is no longer to order and lead worship, preach the Gospel, teach the faith, engage in pastoral care and service according to truth (sound doctrine); rather, their role is to meet the varying needs of the community of faith, which is getting to be a complicated task in psychotherapeutic and pluralistic America.

Naturally, seminaries have already responded and continue to respond to this changing practical reality. Therefore, preparation and training for the ordained ministry is becoming less and less the search for and delighting in the truth and knowledge of God (a theological aim), and more and more the acquisition of practical skills and information to meet the ever-growing demands of modern congregations (a practical aim). Refresher courses—D.Min. degrees—provide clergy with the further skills and information needed to meet the new needs of the present generation of church members. The pursuit of theology as the knowledge of God somehow gets forgotten or, worse still, gets transmuted into modern, secular, practical knowledge of how to manage conflict among competing groups and how to deal with the felt needs of people.

In fact, during the 1970s and even in the 1980s, cultural conflicts could be seen within many traditionally conservative Protestant seminaries. On the Boards of Trustees were a goodly number of the old middle class who believed and hoped that the education and training would provide for the churches the type of pastors and preachers they had known in the 1950s and earlier. This group still believed that ministerial function should grow out of ministerial vocation, as governed by the truth of God provided in sacred Scripture. But on the faculty were a majority from the new class who desired to make theological education relevant to the changing situation in both society at large and the churches in particular. This relevance included their working from the centrality of the cult of personality, with the pastor as the friend of all, ever ready to acquire new skills to function as manager and therapist. In the student body were students raised in the 1960s who wanted to make religion into a viable, experiential reality for their generation. Thus they wanted to know not what is true but what works; not who is God as God, but what does God mean for, and what will He do for, me.

ON INDIVIDUALISM AND COMMUNITY

Liberalism in politics and religion could not have existed and developed without the emergence and growth of what has come to be called individualism. Certainly liberalism could not be a going concern today in the West without the existence of a universal and powerful individualism. (Ironically, the same has to be said of contemporary forms of conservative religion in America—they also flourish in the ethos of modern utilitarian and expressive individualism.) In the seventeenth century there was a sustained call for freedom of conscience in the practice of religion. This may be described as an expression of Protestant individualism; it was inextricably intertwined with the doctrines of justification by faith, the priesthood of all believers, the inner witness of the Holy Spirit in the soul, and the right of private judgment in the reading of Holy Scripture. This individualism was not (in theory) self-centered or self-directed, for it intended to make a man fulfill his duties to God and to mankind. In the nineteenth century both evangelicals and liberal Protestants shared this basic understanding that each man was free to serve God and fulfill his vocation. The residue of this form of biblical individualism is still found in modern people who take seriously the reading of the Scriptures as the written Word of God, a Word to be obeyed.

Different from, but often fused with, Protestant individualism is what has been called a civic or republican individualism. This was to be found particularly in America in the late eighteenth and early nineteenth centuries and is in some ways an idealization of what was supposed to have been the character of the citizens of the Greek city-states in the time of Plato and Aristotle. Thomas Jefferson's first inaugural address in 1801 provides a good example. Each citizen was free, but freedom meant serving the common good and the republic. It was a freedom from the shackles of monarchical and aristocratic government in order to share in the responsibilities and duties of democracy. Freedom meant both privileges and duties in the public sphere. Again, the residue of this civic individualism is found today among those people who have a high sense of public service and commitment.

The word *individualism* was not used of what I have called Protestant individualism and civic individualism until long after they were part of the American experience and memory. In fact, I would prefer not to use the word for what the Puritans and the Founding Fathers both stood for and exhibited; however, since it is so widely used today, I cannot avoid using it of their position (which is better described as responsible, personal freedom). The truth of the matter is that the word *individualism* only entered general vocabulary in the mid-nineteenth century after its use by Alexis de Tocqueville in his *Democracy in America* early in the nineteenth century. He pointed out that *individualism* was a word recently coined (in France and then in America) to express a new idea, an idea similar to but not identical with that which had hitherto been called egoism.

He defined *egoism* as "a passionate and exaggerated love of self that leads a man to think of all things in terms of himself and to prefer himself to all." In contrast, he wrote that *individualism* is "a calm and considered feeling that disposes each citizen to isolate himself from the mass of his fellows and withdraw into the circle of family and friends: with this little society formed to his taste, he gladly leaves the greater society to look after itself." And he further explained that while egoism is a vice as old as the world and is not peculiar to one form of society or another, "individualism is of democratic origin and threatens to grow as conditions get more equal." The tendency of democracy is that each person is thrown back on himself, and there is a danger "that he may be shut up in the solitude of his own heart" (Tocqueville, *Democracy in America*, 477-480)

Obviously, in his journeys around America the observant Tocqueville had noticed a phenomenon that could not be equated with the responsible personal freedom of the early Puritans, the later Founding Fathers, and their successors. Nor could it be found in the monarchical and aristocratic societies of old Europe. Through the study of the history of culture we now know that by the middle of the nineteenth century two forms of what is properly called individualism had developed in Western culture and were particularly evident in America. One has been called "utilitarian individualism," and the other, which is partly a reaction to it, has been called "expressive individualism."

The key to understanding these two modern expressions of individualism is that they arose when it was widely believed that the individual man is prior to a society. That is, a society is the coming together of individual human beings. Political and social unity is that of a social contract. In contrast, the responsible freedom (Protestant and civic individualism) of earlier times thought of society as prior to the individual person. Each person, it was held, was related to others, and his identity arose from the fact of those relationships (not only of blood and affinity but also of the local community). The new ideas, with their basis in the philosophies of John Locke and Jean-Jacques Rousseau, naturally led to (what is the now very common) use of the adjective *individual* to describe a single human being. Further, these ideas quickly led, in the social context of the emergence of the industrial revolution, to a man's believing that what was for his own benefit and that of his family was for the benefit of all—thus utilitarian individualism. We need to add here that such individualism was tempered for a long time in American society by the continuance of the traditions of Protestant and civic individualism and thus was saved from merely being or becoming an excessive form of egoism.

Once the *individual* (notice how an adjective replaces a noun, *man*, in traditional English) had become the center of the emerging democracy and capitalism, then it was to be expected that poets and seers would begin to think that what made each individual person unique was his inner life—his own unique psychology. Hence there emerged expressive individualism, and it was, of course, closely associated with the romantic movement in Europe and America. In reaction to the aridity of reason that emerged from the Enlightenment, there developed an emphasis on the epistemological significance of feelings and emotions. Romanticism retained the emphasis on the individual person from the Enlightenment but supplanted a concern with reason with a new interest in the imagination and inner feelings/emotions/sentiments. The claim was further made that such feeling is oriented toward the eternal, the infinite, and the transcendent. Human subjectivity and inwardness were now perceived as a mirror of the eternal and infinite. (We saw in chapter two how Friedrich Schleiermacher of Berlin was able to build on this foundation to commend the Christian religion to his contemporaries.)

Such feeling is clearly seen, for example, in the influential literature of Novalis (Friedrich von Hardenberg), in *Ideen* by Johann G. Herder, and in *Leaves of Grass* (1897) by the American Walt Whitman. Even the rational, political theorist John Stuart Mill develops its importance in his famous essay *On Liberty*. In addition, the strength of Pietism in Germany and Methodism in England in the eighteenth and early nineteenth century also testify to the cultivation of feelings in the evangelism, fellowship, and worship of evangelicalism. In America, Pietism and Methodism (via revivalism) were even more widely known and experienced. Thereby, the turn to inwardness and to the centrality of feelings became a virtually necessary part of vital religion. Then, from the 1960s with its widespread subjectivist turn in culture and the attendant development of psychotherapy, this expressive form of individualism has become almost the normal kind of individualism for Americans (though again it is often tempered by one or more of the other three forms of individualism and thus is saved from its own inherent excesses).

I was gratified to find that *The American Heritage Dictionary* expresses some hesitancy about the use of *individual* simply as a substitute for *person*:

> *Individual* (noun) in the sense of "a person" is fittingly used when a single human being is distinguished from a group or mass, by contrast or by stress on a special quality: *the individual's right to dissent from a majority view; an individual to the core*. It is not acceptably used . . . according to the majority of the Usage Panel, when it is simply a substitute for *person: two individuals were arrested for the crime*. (1982, 656)

I fear that over the last decade the use of this word simply to mean a person has become very widespread. The individualism in the souls of those speaking English has caused this development.

Limited government, in contrast to modern regulatory government, existed in the early nineteenth century when evangelical Protestantism flourished and when the Protestant and civic forms of individualism were prominent in society. At least in part this explains how education, health, and social welfare were run by voluntary societies in the nineteenth century. People had a sense of duty and service. Modern welfare-regulatory government exists in late twentieth-century society where expressive and utilitarian individualism are dominant. Leonard Sweet explains:

> Since the late nineteenth century, when entrepreneurial capitalism was transformed into corporate capitalism, the individual person has been absorbed into the corporate enterprise. The structural constraints of a competitive free market economy—the constraints to consume, the constraints to produce, the constraints to experience, the constraints to achieve—are just as severe as the controlling attempts of a socialist economy [e.g., as that of the former USSR]. Both pressure humans to feel and think in certain ways: in one system these ways are defined by the state; in the other they are defined by a corporate bureaucracy. . . . The

> power of economics and technology to change individual,
> eccentric behavior into mass, centric behavior is more effec-
> tive than the barrel of a gun. (*Liberal Protestantism*, 240)

At least in part, this explains why the gulf between the public and private spheres grows and religion is seen as belonging to the latter sphere only.

Likewise in the sphere of religion, there is a close relationship between the older forms of evangelical Protestantism/theology and the teaching and practice of responsible freedom, and between the new (particularly post-1960s) forms of liberal Protestantism/theology and the assumptions of modern utilitarian and expressive individualism. At the same time, it cannot be denied that utilitarian and expressive individualism have made major inroads into modern conservative, evangelical religion, where they seem to co-exist with a basic biblical individualism.

In fact, I cannot see how it is possible to make much sense of either the variety of contemporary liberal, secular theologies or the popular so-called biblical teaching of the television evangelists and preachers without recognizing how deeply embedded modern individualism is in both camps. For example, the individualism resident in liberalism's pedigree has united with pluralism in society to create the assumption—even doctrine—that everyone has a right to do whatever she or he wants to do. Fundamentals of the old liberal theology such as freedom, equality, and justice have been stripped of their fuller meaning—even as the older support for civil rights in the 1960s has degenerated into support for special-interest groups where rights tend to mean self-fulfillment and self-gratification. Within evangelicalism, individualism can often be seen in the portrayal of salvation as an individualistic relationship with God, as a this-worldly sense of happiness and success, and as a mere extension of middle-class, bourgeois culture.

Moreover, this individualistic mind-set is reflected in the near universal use by both liberals and conservatives of the word *community* to describe the local Christian congregation. Behind this usage is, of course, the idea of the priority of the individual's freely choosing to belong to and become a part of this or that voluntary society (i.e., community). In terms of modern Western society this union of individual and community seems to make good sense. As a result, however, the local church as community is less an experience of wholeness, relatedness, and authenticity in God's presence and more an experience of the affirming and even celebration of segmentation, simulation, and atomization in each other's presence.

In his important book *The Denial of Death* (1973), Ernest Becker has shown that each of us experiences two internal urges, motives, and pulls in apparently opposite directions. First of all, there is the deep desire to be a part of something larger than oneself (family, tribe, clan, community, and so forth). In the second place, there is the inescapable urge to stand apart from everyone else in order to be oneself and be different. This twin attraction and repulsion means that modern people must do the impossible—choose between the cultivation of the self and the search for community. Often to keep themselves from going mad they need therapy! If the church merely seeks to be the answer to the search for community and presents religion in terms of individualism, then it is functioning (primarily horizontally) as one part of society. Only when it seeks to fulfill its high calling (vertically—Godward) to be the body of Christ and the household of faith and to offer friendship with God in a personal relation with the Father through the Son and in the Holy Spirit will it be able to allow God to minister to His creatures for their good in this world and the world to come.

Apparently, today it is only the very traditional Protestant, Roman Catholic, and Greek Orthodox believers who seem to hesitate to speak of the church of God as a community. This is because their language of worship and faith comes from the Bible and from pre-Enlightenment liturgical texts and traditions in which the concept of modern individualism is not present. Of course, not to use the language of modern individualism does not mean to say that the reality is not present in the souls of the faithful.

TRANSITIONS

Professor Jürgen Moltmann of Tübingen has noted that the general environment in which theology is being pursued in the latter part of the twentieth century is one characterized by a transition in three major areas. First, there is a transition from a denominational or confessional context (e.g., Lutheran) to an ecumenical context. Because of the influence of the World Council of Churches and the ecumenical movement, there is a migration within university departments of theology from particularist to universalist thinking. This goes hand in hand with a recognition that the concerns and problems of other churches are one's own also. In addition, there is a convergence in the production of new liturgies for denominations within the ecumenical movement. People today notice that the structure of the basic service is the same in the Roman, Anglican, and Methodist churches, for example.

Second, there is a transition from the Eurocentric age to the whole-of-humanity age. The center of gravity for theology is no longer to be found in Western churches and universities; it is to be found wherever the Spirit (of God or of the age?) is moving the churches into new insights and action for the kingdom of God. Related to this transition is the move away from the domination of male, Caucasian, patriarchal, androcentric forms of thinking to thinking that is more representative of the whole of humanity, including women and other minorities. Naturally connected with such thinking is not only the call for the use of inclusive language for human beings and perhaps also for God but also an attempt to present a new, up-to-date theology of the Spirit of God, active in human culture and human consciousness.

Finally, there is a transition from the age of mechanistic domination of the world to the age of ecological, world-wide community. Technology has always been used without concern for the long-term good of the planet; now there is an awakening to the need to be faithful stewards of the creation. "What is needed is not the secularization of the world but its sacralization; not the legitimation of human domination of nature [through technology] but the incorporation of humanity in the universe" (Moltmann, "Theology in Transition," 223).

So Moltmann believes that a truly contemporary theology is needed and is emerging. It cannot be the same as its parentage or its grandparentage because the total environment, and our way of looking at it, are so different now than only three decades ago. And if theology is to be relevant and meaningful in the present age, this context and environment must be recognized and addressed. Moltmann himself is known as a pioneer of a theology of hope, in which God is the God of the future, to whom we move. This theology had a major impact in the 1960s on the creation of the new liberation theologies of South America and the Third World.

ASPECTS OF CRISIS

Professor Hans Küng, the well-known Roman Catholic ecumenist, has worked hard to get modern theologians to cooperate in the theological task. After an international conference in Tübingen, Germany, he sought to summarize the various contributions from his European and American colleagues as to the content or the characteristics of the crisis that they all believed theology as a discipline was facing in the modern world. All the papers are collected in *Paradigm Change in Theology* (1989), which he edited with David Tracy. Küng's own paper is summarized below.

In the first place, he greeted the end of four hundred years of Western (European and American) political and military, economic and cultural hegemony and the emergence and development of other centers of power (e.g., Japan). The buzz word for this new phenomenon is *polycentricism*. Thus, theologians cannot any longer think merely as either westerners or easterners who are locked into their cultural skins. They are citizens of the whole world who must see through and beyond their cultural horizons. This means that all must put forth a tremendous effort to appreciate and think with other cultures than one's own.

In the second place, Küng pointed to the profound ambiguity found in modern science, technology, and industrialization because they each can be potentially both destructive and creative—to destroy or to renew the environment. Therefore theologians, in discussing God's creation and the human vocation in the world, must address this ambiguity, make people aware of it, and offer advice as to an appropriate use of such powerful forces.

In the third place, he referred to the social antagonism found in the First as well as in the Third World, and expressed in exploitation and repression, as well as in racism and sexism. This, he insisted, is a major challenge to Christian thinkers who believe that all human beings, men and women, are made in the image of God. Obviously, theological writing ought not to serve social antagonism but point to harmony and reconciliation. It ought to be sensitive to the needs of women and minorities and affirm their place in God's world and kingdom.

In the fourth place, he noted that there has been a shaking of the foundations of the symbols that underpin modern, Western culture. In particular the myth of progress in all fields—scientific and social, industrial and political—has been (or is being) generally abandoned, and in its place has come a general pessimism about the future, together with a lack of orientation in the present. It is up to theologians to reinterpret the Christian hope not only of the world to come, but also of God's presence and activity in this world and age.

In the fifth place, he highlighted the changed (changing) position of the book, the role of the university, and the place of theology as one of the human sciences. All are endangered by opposing pressures: hypermodern differentiation and specialization, individualism and pluralism. Therefore, the theologian cannot think, write, and publish in the way that his own teachers did—sitting as they did on a pedestal, looking down on the world. He has to be aware of the context in which knowledge is sought and disseminated today and adapt the message and the means of communicating it to the modern social and economic reality. This, of course, is easier said than done, especially in a world in which communication is dominated by the images on the television screen.

In the sixth place, the loss of Western dominance in the world has also meant the undermining of the claim of Christianity to be the one, true religion. Now Christianity and other religions compete on equal footing in many parts of the world. So theologians today have to take dialogue with adherents of other religions seriously, being ready to listen to and learn from them.

Finally, the great catastrophes of modern times (e.g., Auschwitz, Hiroshima, the Gulag Archipelago, and mass starvation in Africa) serve to show that idealistic constructions of history can no longer be written. Theologians must take account of human suffering and create an option for the poor. Also, they must take into account the suffering of women over the centuries and seek to incorporate the new consciousness of women's vocation and destiny into their thinking.

Küng is fond of the word *paradigm* (basic model) to communicate what he understands doing theology to be. His goal is a plural theology—that is, a cluster of theologies open to learn from and ready to discuss with each other because all will be done within a common general context of understanding. So he wrote:

> A number of different theologies are possible within the one post-Enlightenment, post-modern paradigm, or basic model. Different theological trends, schools and locations compete for the best way of shaping the paradigm, its presuppositions and consequences. A hermeneutical and a political theology, a process theology, and all the different expressions and trends of liberation theology (feminist, black or third-world)

can co-exist and compete within the bounds of a contemporary post-Enlightenment, post-modern paradigm of a Christian (ecumenical) theology. At all events, the new paradigm needs the world-wide political perspective and this means that the different continents (not merely Latin America) and religions (not merely Christianity) must all be taken into account. (*Paradigm Change in Theology*, 451)

It hardly needs to be added that within this paradigm there is no place for traditional Eastern Orthodox, Roman Catholic, or Protestant theology, for they are neither post-Enlightenment nor postmodern in method or content.

While Küng may be said to represent an advanced position, there is nevertheless something to be said for the view that doing theology today is unlike doing it in any other period. Avery Dulles, S.J., a more conservative Roman Catholic than is Küng, writes:

Labels such as "postmodern," "postliberal," and "postcritical" are likely to be rather manipulative. They seem to put unfair demands on people to conform to what the speaker proclaims as the spirit of the age, with the implication that previous approaches are obsolete. But at the same time the prevalence of such terminology indicates a widespread perception that we are moving, or have already moved, into a period radically unlike the past few centuries, necessitating an abrupt shift of theological style comparable in magnitude to the shift that occurred with the dissemination of printed literature in the sixteenth century. Without wishing to exaggerate the discontinuity, I share this perception to some degree. (*The Craft of Theology*, 1992, 3)

In fact, many people appear to share this perception to a lesser or greater degree.

A SOCIAL PORTRAIT OF THE THEOLOGIAN

David Tracy of Chicago begins his *Analogical Imagination: Christian Theology and the Culture of Pluralism* (1981) with this claim: "Theologians not only recognize a plurality of 'publics' to whom they intend to speak, but also more and more the theologians are internalizing this plurality in their own discourse. The results are often internal confusion and external chaos" (3). His view is that the pluralism of cultural worlds has enriched us all with new visions of our common lives and new possibilities for an authentic life.

Within this pluralism each theologian addresses three distinct and socially related groups—the wider society, the academy, and the church. Of course, in practice a particular book is usually addressed primarily to one group. However, this does not mean that it, in a secondary or partially hidden way, is not addressed to the others as well. For this reason the theologian today has to be aware of these three publics.

Living in a modern, complex society, the theologian needs to reflect on the structures and culture of that society, for he is affected by it in all kinds of ways. He ought not to be pushed into or gravitate toward the insulated and marginalized sphere of a religious subculture, believing he has no word for his fellow citizens in the larger society. What he has to say should be available to all, not merely to a restrictive minority.

Being an academic and working within the general provisions and assumptions of the academy, the theologian must have (or be aware of) proposals for the actual place for theology as a viable discipline within the modern university. With this will need to go a particular method for doing theology that will command the attention of serious, fellow professionals in related disciplines.

As a member of the church (the community of moral and religious discourse), the theologian addresses it from within but understands it both as a sociological and also as a theological reality. Tracy insists that "unlike participation in a family, participation in a church is now a strictly voluntary matter. Anyone may leave or join at any time" (21). The theologian must bear this in mind and talk and write accordingly.

Thus, it is not only the fact of living within and addressing three publics, but it is also the fact of having internalized the three publics that characterizes the modern situation. The theologian, being a human being, cannot escape the unconscious formation of his thought and attitudes by the three publics. And in addressing one of them he speaks as one who is already affected not only by that public but by the other two also.

In summary, to do theology in the modern, Western world, the sociological reality of the three publics must be recognized both in their external realities and in their internal appropriation. This places heavy demands on and offers great rewards to theologians.

For Tracy, as a Roman Catholic, there are three disciplines within theology—fundamental, systematic, and practical. Fundamental theology speaks primarily to the academy, providing arguments for belief in the God of Jesus Christ. It makes use of philosophy and may even be called philosophical theology. Systematic theology speaks primarily to the church as the community of moral and religious discourse and action. It explores, re-presents, and reinterprets the holy tradition of Christianity and is principally hermeneutical in character. Finally, practical theology speaks primarily to society at large and with reference to some particular social, political, cultural, or pastoral movement or problem. It assumes that praxis (the situation on the ground), and involvement in it to bring transformation, is the proper criterion for meaning and truth. Though each discipline has a primary reference, it will speak to the other publics directly or indirectly as well.

REFLECTIONS

There is no doubt that the theological grandchildren of nineteenth-century parents have taken into their personalities many, if not all, of the environmental factors mentioned above. Of course, each child has absorbed the factors in different ways and degrees according to his situation and context. For example, for obvious reasons feminist theology has made more of the claimed deprivations and suffering of women as women than has black theology; but black theology has made more of the discrimination against and suffering of blacks as blacks (female or male) than has feminist theology; and process theology has made more of the doctrine of cosmic evolution than has narrative theology.

There is little doubt that any modern theology that desires truly to be *contemporary* faces challenges that are political, scientific, economic, religious, social, and cultural. Further, the way theologians face these challenges determines how they do their theological thinking. Referring specifically to the challenge faced by modern Roman Catholic theologians, Professor Schüssler Fiorenza of Harvard Divinity School writes:

> If theologians assess the present situation as secularized, as being characterized by the absence of past moral values and the demise of traditional religious meanings, then they view the retrieval of these values and the reactualization of these meanings as the paramount theological task. If they place the political, social and racial oppressions in the forefront, then overcoming these oppressions is a major goal of theology. If they take human alienation or personal inauthenticity to be the basic problem, then the attainment of authenticity and the overcoming of alienation are the primary goals. (*Systematic Theology*, 1991, 1:66)

Much the same can be said, of course, of modern Protestant theology. It is certainly true that the position and assumptions from which one starts affect the way the theology is done and to which public it is primarily addressed.

FOR FURTHER READING, GENERAL

Berger, Peter L. "Different Gospels: The Social Sources of Apostasy." In *Apostate America: The Triumph of Different Gospels*. Edited by Richard Neuhaus. Grand Rapids, Mich.: Eerdmans, 1988.

_____. *Facing up to Modernity: Excursions in Society, Politics and Religion*. New York: Basic, 1977.

_____. *The Heretical Imperative: Contemporary Possibilities of Religious Affirmation*. Garden City, N.Y.: Doubleday, 1979.

Dulles, Avery, J. S. *The Craft of Theology: From Symbol to System.* New York: Crossroad, 1992.

Guinness, Os. *The American Hour, A Time of Reckoning and the Once and Future Role of Faith.* New York: Free Press, 1992.

Johnson, Paul. *Modern Times: From the Twenties to the Nineties.* Rev. ed. New York: HarperCollins, 1991.

Küng, Hans. "A New Basic Model for Theology: Divergencies and Convergencies." In *Paradigm Change in Theology. A Symposium for the Future.* Edited by Hans Kung and David Tracy. New York: Crossroad, 1989.

Moltmann, Jürgen. "Theology in Transition—To What?" in *Paradigm Change in Theology. A Symposium for the Future.* Edited by Hans Kung and David Tracy. New York: Crossroad, 1989.

Rief, Philip. *The Triumph of the Therapeutic.* Chicago: University of Chicago Press, 1987.

Simmons, John K. "Complementism: Liberal Protestant Potential within a Fully Realized Cultural Environment." In *Liberal Protestantism.* Edited by Robert S. Michaelsen and Wade C. Roof. New York: Pilgrim Press, 1986.

Tracy, David. *The Analogical Imagination: Christian Theology and the Culture of Pluralism.* New York: Crossroad, 1981.

FOR FURTHER READING, ON INDIVIDUALISM

Arieli, Yehoshua. *Individualism and Nationalism in American Ideology.* Cambridge, Mass.: Harvard University Press, 1964.

Bellah, Robert N., et al., eds. *Habits of the Heart: Individualism and Commitment in American Life.* Berkeley, Calif.: University of California Press, 1985.

———. *Individualism and Commitment in American Life: Readings on the Themes of "Habits of the Heart."* New York: Harper & Row, 1987.

Durkheim, Emile. "Individualism and the Intellectuals." In

Durkheim on Religion. Edited by W. S. Pickering. Boston: Routledge and Kegan Paul, 1975.

Hunter, James Davison. *American Evangelicalism: Conservative Religion and the Quandary of Modernity.* New Brunswick, N.J.: Rutgers University Press, 1983.

MacIntyre, Alasdair. *After Virtue.* South Bend, Ind.: University of Notre Dame Press, 1981.

Stuart, Koenraad W. "Individualism in the Mid-nineteenth Century." *Journal of the History of Ideas* 23 (1962): 77-95.

Sweet, Leonard. "Can a Mainstream Change Its Course?" In *Liberal Protestantism: Realities and Possibilities.* Edited by Robert S. Michaelsen and Wade Clark Roof. New York: Pilgrim, 1986.

Taylor, Charles. *Sources of the Self.* Cambridge, Mass.: Harvard University Press, 1989.

Tocqueville, Alexis de. *Democracy in America.* Translated by George Lawrence. Edited by J. P. Mayer. New York: Doubleday, 1969.

APPENDIX: MAJOR INFLUENCES ON ROMAN CATHOLIC THEOLOGY

After the Second Vatican Council (1962-65), Bernard Lonergan, S.J., looked back over earlier decades to note what had been the major influences involved in the changing nature of Roman Catholic theology from a deductive to an empirical method. In "Theology and Man's Future" in *Second Collection* (1974) he examined five areas.

First, "one of the profoundest changes ... has been brought about by modern methods of historical study" (135). That is, the historical-critical method has made a great impact both on the study of the development of doctrine in history and also within the Scriptures.

Second, the historical ties with the philosophy of Aristotle and Thomas Aquinas have been loosened and broken.

"Contemporary theologians are drawing upon personal, phenomenological, existential, historical and transcendental types of philosophical thought to find the conceptual tools needed for their own thinking and writing" (137).

Third, the new field of religious studies has been very influential is providing a different ethos for study. He has in mind the disciplines of the phenomenology of religion, the sociology of religion, the history of religions, and the philosophy of religions. Each of these is a modern approach to the study of Christianity and other religions, and all together have been gaining ground in recent years.

Fourth is the area of methodology. Instead of being wedded to the notion of science as developed by Aristotle and Thomas Aquinas, modern Catholic theologians have accepted modern ways of defining and understanding what science is. Thus, theology as a science means something rather different for them than it did in the period of neo-Scholasticism. For one thing, even as the modern scientist is an expert in only one basic area (e.g., an aspect of physics), even so the theologian cannot claim to synthesize all knowledge; he too must be a specialist in one area.

Finally, there is the need to communicate the faith in a modern world, and this has caused theologians to examine how they write. There is no longer one dominant and normative culture in the Western world as earlier centuries could claim. Today culture is an empirical category, for modern culture knows many cultures, which it studies and compares. Culture as a category knows that cultures are man-made and subject to development and decay. Accordingly, communication in this condition of relativity and flux is very different from what neo-Scholasticism had presumed.

Lonergan recognizes that there were other formative influences for change, but he insists these five areas are the important ones for assessing the changes in Catholic theology.

Chapter 4

The 1960s

There is a general agreement that the 1960s was a momentous time in the Western world and especially in North America. Perhaps future historians will judge it to be of as great a significance as were the American Revolution and the Civil War for the development of American culture. Certainly, such old foundations as patriotic idealism, national confidence, traditional morality, and biblical theism were severely shaken, challenged, changed, or even abandoned. The winds of modernity blew at gale force and affected virtually all institutions, not least the old-line Protestant denominations.

To prepare our minds to understand modern theologies we shall reflect on the 1960s. Then, with this general context in mind, we shall look at a book entitled *Honest to God*, published in a small edition in early 1963 in England. Its author, John Robinson, the bishop of Woolwich, anticipated that he would be accused of being radical and heretical by fellow scholars, but neither he nor his publishers expected the book's bombshell effect on the mass of ordinary readers. In just a few months *Honest to God* was a runaway best seller and available in nine languages. On both sides of the Atlantic the book provoked debate and discussion, ranging almost from ecstasy to deepest anguish and condemnation. It is a safe assumption that a best seller tells more about the market than the product, and this was true with *Honest to God*. Probably at no other time than the early 1960s could such a book have had such a phenomenal success.

Indeed, this book brought to the notice of many people the names of three theologians—Rudolf Bultmann, Dietrich Bonhoeffer, and Paul Tillich—who had deeply influenced Robinson, and who also were to be very influential in theological education and discussion in the 1960s. So we shall also look briefly at what these German-born theologians taught. Finally, we shall notice two further theologies that came into prominence in the late 1960s—process theology and the theology of hope, both of which helped pave the way for various liberation theologies of the 1970s.

THE TWO 1960s

On January 3, 1994, *Newsweek* provided descriptions of each decade of the twentieth century from the thirties to the nineties. Under the heading "The '60s: Tornado of Wrath," the article began:

> The '60s split the skies. Only the Civil and two world wars so neatly clove our history into a Before and After. And the '60s were more divisive than World War II, which drew people together for the war effort. The '60s drove people apart—husbands from wives, children from parents, students from teachers, citizens from their government. Authority was strengthened by World War II. It was challenged by the '60s.

It proceeded to see much good arising from the "tornado of wrath" and claimed rather dubiously that "the '60s play the same role in conservative political thought that the Fall of Man does in Christian theology."

For a more balanced study of the 1960s from a religious perspective we turn to an essay by Leonard I. Sweet under the title, "The 1960s: The Crises of Liberal Christianity and the Public Emergence of Evangelicalism." He argues that there were really two "sixties." The first (roughly from 1960 to 1967) was bursting with belief, fresh hope, and high ambition; the second (roughly from 1967 to 1971) was comprised of polar opposites with broken dreams, worn-out emotions, shattered institutions, fragmented selves, and failed communes.

At the beginning of the 1960s the old-line denominations (Presbyterian, Episcopalian, and so forth) provided a major part of the vital center of American life and morals. However, the way in which these churches came to terms with the questions of authority raised in the first sixties "led to a profound loss of Protestant identity and consequent evacuation of meaning, confusion of purpose, and frustration of mission in American religious life" (Sweet, "The 1960s . . . ," 31). For the first time the authority of the church was widely discredited in American religion. Instead of the churches' being seen as the institutions that set the standards for society, they were increasingly seen as being there to meet the needs of society. This was a remarkable and far-reaching change.

It was not that there were no authorities in the first sixties. There was, however, a turning from ecclesiastical to cultural authorities, from the Bible and tradition to the new *Zeitgeist* (spirit of the age). Sweet thinks that the best example of this trend was the great enthusiasm for relativism in morals, known as situation ethics. The so-called new morality taught that all you bring to a moral situation is "love" (love was defined more by the culture than by the Bible). Liberation comes when you forget the bondage of the Ten Commandments and simply bring love into the situation, for each situation is unique and autonomous. An Episcopalian, Joseph Fletcher, wrote the book, *Situation Ethics* (1966), which came to reflect this thinking.

But why did the churches dismantle religious authority and so quickly accept cultural authority? Sweet suggests several reasons. First of all, there was a deep desire not to be out of touch but to be with it. So, whatever seemed alien to the modern mind had to go, and all that was not felt to be meaningful had to be dropped. To change, and to change quickly, was the order of the day; and thus *new* was one of the pet words of that time. Sweet remarks that "whereas an older liberalism had capitulated to the authority of the modern scientific world view, the liberalizing trend that characterized religion in the first sixties capitulated to the authority of a broader and more encompassing phenomenon of cultural secularization" (ibid., 34).

Second, there was an enthusiastic embrace of secularity: the process of secularization was seen as being part of the general providence of God. To cling to tradition was seen as holding on to a past that was gone forever. And it was in this spirit that the secular theology of the sixties was produced, of which *The Secular City* (1965) by Harvey Cox is a pertinent example. Cox argued that the process of secularization (guided by the transcendent God) had liberated man from the old supernatural images and made him free to create his own secular myths in and through which he could live consistently in a technological world. Further, as Sweet remarks, "the dethroning of traditional religious authority and the brandishing of Christianity's secular connection were seen as incitements to social action" (ibid.). Christianity, for many people, meant flocking to the picket line to support civil rights or to protest the Vietnam war.

Third, it was held that the old theological mold had cracked beyond repair, and a new mold (cultural authority) was immediately required. Relativism and pluralism (often as egalitarianism) were embraced as the necessary expressions of this mold. Thus, there were no obviously final answers to the really important questions about life because God was dead. That is, the God of Christian or Jewish theism had been a projection of the imagination. Jesus as a man for others was fine, but God was a problem. The theological trend became to speak of Christian atheism as expressed in the writings of William Hamilton, Paul Van Buren, and Thomas Altizer (concerning whom see below).

Fourth, the church as an institution was seen as being irrelevant to modern life and an impediment to social change. The mandate of the clergymen and the theologian was to be loyal not to the tradition of his church but to the experience of love in the totality of human experience. In effect, theology was divorced from the churches, and it effectively became sociology, anthropology, and psychology; also, the Bible became a closed book. In the second sixties, when no distinct identity arose out of the new cultural authorities, there was confusion. Ambiguity and uncertainty were proclaimed as values. Inner sources of the self were affirmed as the ultimate authorities, and America came the closest in its history to suffering a national nervous breakdown. Instead of the decade having been the golden sixties, it was seen in 1971 as the decade when almost everything went wrong.

Since external authorities were discredited or lost, there was a turn inward to the self for authorization. It became fashionable and acceptable to speak of self-love, self-affirmation, and self-acceptance. One had to know self-love before one could love God and other people. Psychologists, psychoanalysts, and psychotherapists came into their own. Expressions of the self as the new authority meant there were movements of self-help, self-discovery, and self-realization. Subjectivism was also seen in the turn to Eastern religions and Eastern meditation, in an increase of the charismatic movement, and in the priority of feelings. "Get in touch with your feelings" became common advice. The pastor had to become the therapist.

Where authority was not grounded in the self and subjectivism, it was centered in human relations. New theories of management or styles of organization were developed and accepted by the churches, and the pastor had to become the manager. Many found in goals and objectives a way of recovering the authority of religion without having to accept the seeming arbitrariness of that authority. Sweet remarks that

> the attempt to redirect ecclesiastical authority from the creeds, traditions, and offices of the church to human relations through a theology of church administration governed all the structural retooling that conventional Protestantism underwent in the beginning of the second sixties. (Ibid., 39)

What was known as the church-management movement was the most significant call to order issued by conventional Protestantism after the chaos and bedlam of the previous vandalism of the faith. From it has come, it may be claimed, the centralized bureaucracies of the denominations.

The turn inward, along with the association with others in reaching for goals and objectives, led to a crisis of identity and, for the first time in human history, the belief in a right to identity. The call was heard that society must be reformed in order to guarantee a sense of worth to every person. This was not a call for freedom of speech or for better economic conditions. Rather, it was a call for a right to identity. Individual persons wanted an answer to the question, who am I? with provision for working out the answer in society.

Historically, personal identity had been established by a sense of coherence (being a part of settled culture that gave meaning to life), a sense of commitment (a conscious belonging to a settled family, church, and community), and continuity (having a sense of roots in a family, community, and church tradition). All three had been shaken by the first sixties, and so in the second sixties there was a crisis of self-identity and the search to recover what previously had been taken for granted in a very different cultural context. So the call for community and *koinonia* became trendy items in the 1970s, for only in and with others could the individual self find identity and affirmation.

Replacing the theology of Christian atheism, the teaching that God is dead and Jesus is his prophet, was the theology of hope. We may see it as a natural successor to the theology of the death of God, for it spoke of a God not available in the present but waiting for us in the future. Furthermore, it provided a way for discouraged and depressed Christians to forget the disappointments of the present and past, take up the cause of the future, and still believe in God.

To date, we have only spoken of the effect of the 1960s on the liberal churches. Conservative Protestantism, which had been pushed out of the center of American life by liberal Protestantism and neo-orthodoxy since the turn of the century, saw its opportunity at the end of the second sixties. During the 1970s, evangelicalism emerged as the dominant force in

American religion. Once again a message of absolute truths, moral standards, and a message of heaven and hell had attraction for many people. However, evangelicals who proclaimed the absolutes had lived through and had been affected by the 1960s, especially in the cultivation of subjectivism, the concern for social action, and the call for community. Indeed, their general appeal was from a platform of a fusion of both traditionalism and modernity, and for a time they were very successful. Yet, as has been noted earlier, evangelicals did not speak with one voice, and their triumph did not last long.

HONEST TO GOD

By the 1960s, many clergy and some laity of the churches in Britain (particularly the Church of England, the Church of Scotland, and the Methodist and Congregational Churches) had been affected in their thinking and attitudes by three movements for reform—the biblical-theology, liturgical, and ecumenical movements. The first had helped them retain the centrality of the Bible and its teaching while accepting higher criticism; the second had made them conscious of the need to make worship meaningful and relevant; and the third had given them a sense of belonging to a whole larger than their own denomination. Much the same could be claimed for the old-line denominations in America.

However, these movements hardly addressed questions of truth—Who is God? and What is the Gospel?—for people who were very conscious of living in a scientific age. Thus, there developed in Britain, among those who wanted to express the faith in ways appropriate to a scientific age (and significantly in the early sixties), what was called Christian radicalism. John Robinson, former Cambridge don and then bishop of Woolwich, called himself a radical and explained what Christian radicalism was in a BBC radio broadcast in February 1963. Its essence, he said, was summed up in the statement of Jesus that "the Sabbath was made for man and not man for the Sabbath."

A radical is neither a reformist nor a revolutionary, although he will have something in common with both. The church always needs both reformists and revolutionaries, but it also needs (especially in troublesome times) the radicals.

The radical seeks to go to the root of the matter. He asks (as it were): What is the Sabbath for? What human values does it exist to frame? Then the radical attempts to ensure (at whatever cost to the institution or to orthodoxy) that it answers the questions. Thus, the radical goes to the roots of his own tradition. He must love that tradition, and he must weep over it, even if he has ultimately to pronounce its doom.

Therefore, the bishop's short book *Honest to God*, explaining his involvement in a reluctant revolution, is an expression of this British radicalism. It is an attempt in the atmosphere of growing secularization to get down to the roots of the tradition found in Scripture and in the history of Christian theology. He challenged traditional ways of thinking about God and God's relation to the world, about the identity of Jesus Christ as both God and man, about Christian morality, and about Christian prayer. He spoke of God as "the ground of Being," of Jesus as "the Man for others," of "the new morality" (nothing prescribed except to love), and of a form of "worldly holiness." And he quoted much from both Tillich and Bonhoeffer as well as referring approvingly to Bultmann's famous essay from the 1940s, "The New Testament and Mythology."

Much water has flowed under the bridge during the thirty years since *Honest to God* first appeared. What seemed outrageous, heretical, and intolerable to the traditional churchgoers in 1963 probably seems commonplace now, even though they did not like it when it was first published. On March 22, 1963, the retired bishop of London, Dr. J. W. C. Wand, summarized the argument of *Honest to God* in these words in his review in *Church Times*:

> The spacemen have searched the skies and have failed to find either the Christian heaven or the God who was supposed to dwell there. The result has been to make our traditional way

of thinking of God as someone "out there" quite outmoded. If we wish to keep in line with modern scientific thought we must think of God as someone "in here" at the root of our being, or, better still, not as being at all but as the ground of all being. It is believed that this will involve a radical re-thinking not only of Christian doctrine but also of worship and ethics. Worship will belong not to some special department of life, but to all life: to work is to pray as to pray is to work. Conduct will be regulated not by a set of rules given from outside, but by the need of love as the very spring of all our actions. However, just as it is necessary to retain the name God in spite of the erosion of the personal element in describing the divine existence, so the rules and regulations are maintained in spite of the blunting of their fine edges by emphasis on the exceptions. (*The Honest to God Debate*, 85)

To Dr. Wand there was not really anything new in what his younger colleague was saying. He hoped, however, that the radical bishop would not continue to attack religion because, for the "man in the street," public worship in the churches was an access to the possibility of faith.

Writing in the [London] *Observer* of Sunday, March 24, 1963, and claiming to speak on behalf of the laity, Professor C. S. Lewis (whose books commending Christian orthodoxy maintained good sales) stated that

we have long abandoned belief in a God who sits on a throne in a localized heaven. We call that belief anthropomorphism, and it was officially condemned before our time. . . . We have always thought of God as being not only "in" and "above", but also "below" us.

Then Lewis proceeded (with tongue in cheek?) to attempt to defend the bishop's position:

The image of the Earth-Mother gets in something which that of the Sky-Father leaves out. Religions of the Earth-Mother have hitherto been spiritually inferior to those of the Sky-Father, but, perhaps, it is now time to readmit some of their elements. (*The Honest to God Debate*, 91)

Lewis's words seem to have a prophetic ring about them as we look back through the years during which we have seen the arrival of Christian feminism and the calling of God "Mother."

While the bishop's fellow radicals enthusiastically commended his theology, one (now well known) writer, Alasdair MacIntyre, then an Oxford don, claimed that the second half of the book revealed that the bishop was "a very conservative atheist." Further, after commenting on the theologies of Tillich, Bultmann, and Bonhoeffer as utilized by the bishop, MacIntyre asserted: "we can see now that Dr. Robinson's voice is not just that of an individual, that his book testifies to the existence of a whole group of theologies that have retained a theistic vocabulary but acquired an atheistic substance" (*Encounter*, September 1963, in *The Honest to God Debate*, 215). MacIntyre spoke from within the British school of the philosophy of language. According to that school's use of the verification principle, the bishop did not speak of God at all.

In America, Theodore O. Wedel of the Cathedral of St. John the Divine, New York, explained in *The Episcopalian* of August 1963:

> The Bishop of Woolwich is not committing a crime in revealing to a wider public what has been going on for a generation and longer in the world of advanced theological learning. He is attempting to prepare the laity of the churches for readjustments in some of their naive, adolescent, often outdated, and even idolatrous conceptions of the Christian faith. It is the business of our theologians to reinterpret the faith to each age of cultural change. *Honest to God* is simply a bold and, as some theologians may say, premature opening of a Pandora's box of theological novelties under debate among doctors of the schools behind the scenes. (*The Honest to God Debate*, 180)

Dr. Wedel believed that the churches were in the midst of a Copernican revolution and it was necessary for them to adjust to it for survival.

In the late fall of 1963, when the dust had settled and the initial reviews had been written and published, the bishop collected his thoughts, and they were published as the concluding part of the book, *The Honest to God Debate*. In certain ways what the bishop wrote here is clearer than what he wrote in the book that led to all the excitement and debate.

Dr. Robinson used the analogy of a currency crisis (e.g., of the pound sterling) to seek to portray what had happened from March 1963. His book played a major part in causing a crisis regarding confidence in the value of traditional, orthodox Christian discourse—in the creeds, doctrinal formulations, moral codes, and liturgical forms. The crisis centered on the questions: Are the doctrinal statements (e.g., "I believe in God the Father Almighty . . .") to be understood objectively or subjectively? Do the creeds describe God as God truly is—the eternal, infinite Being, who causes all being—or do they describe God (the Ground of Being) as we experience it/Him?

The bishop certainly held that doctrinal statements are much more the result of reflection on religious experience than they are objective descriptions of God and supernature.

> To stress this existential, experiential element behind all the Christian's affirmations is not in the least to say that they are purely subjective, in the sense that they represent merely his way of looking at things. . . . They are expressions of a trust in a Reality which is trust-worthy; and the clauses of the Creed, the doctrines and forms of the Church, describe this Reality, not just the individual's state. But they are subjective in the sense in which Kierkegaard said that "Truth is subjectivity." For truth beyond the level of information cannot, he insisted, be apprehended in a purely objective, "spectator" relationship, but only as man is prepared to stand, as subject in an I-Thou relationship of engagement, trust, and commitment. It is in this sense that Tillich can say that "all theological statements are existential": they have all in the last resort to be referred back to this relationship, and their cash value tested by it. (*The Honest to God Debate*, 244)

Even as in times of prosperity we do not much think about what lies behind our paper money, so likewise in normal times churchgoers do not ask about and question the doctrinal statements of the church. In 1963, said Dr. Robinson, they were asking whether such discourse stood for anything *real*. What is its cash value?

When there is a currency crisis there are basically two ways of reacting. One is to stress the value of the old money, engage in appropriate reforms, and try to extend its area of exchange. The other is to admit that the old money has a limited life and to set about seeing how it can be replaced, while there is time, by another currency with as little real loss as may be managed. In the theological-currency crisis, Dr. Robinson, as a Christian radical, insisted that Christians should not fear the crisis but face it honestly and openly—which he was seeking to do. He sincerely believed that the process of secularization, with its distrust of any proposition's going beyond the empirical evidence, was forcing the church to strip down its statements and be rigorously honest about what it could claim.

The way in which the bishop explains the doctrine of the Trinity indicates clearly what he means by a radical restatement of classic orthodoxy.

> The doctrine of the Trinity is not, as it has often been represented, a model of the divine life as it is in itself. It is a formula or definition describing the distinctively Christian encounter with God. Hence all the features in the Trinitarian formula are in the last analysis representations of elements in the existential relationship. (Ibid., 254)

The Christian experience, he insists, is of one God in three modes of being, and yet they are not simply successive modes. So,

> positively, one can say that for the Christian the deepest awareness of ultimate reality, of what for him is most truly and finally real, can only be described at one and the same time in terms of the love of God and of the grace of our Lord Jesus Christ and of the fellowship of the Holy Spirit. All these are equally true and equally deep insights into and understanding of reality, and yet they palpably express and define one reality, not competing realities. (Ibid., 255)

Yet, the doctrine of the Trinity is not the description of *a* or *the* specific, supernatural Being as He exists in his own eternity and infinity. Rather, it is the description of Being as Being (not *a* or *the* Being) known in and through Jesus Christ. Thus, the doctrine or dogma is to the experienced reality of Being what the map is to the earth or the model is to the scientist. The truths of this doctrine are truths about the relational experience in and with Being and are readings from it; they are not statements about God-as-God-is-in-Himself, for that presumes an untenable view of God for modern man. Humanity has left behind the three-deckered universe and cannot think of a great chain of being beginning with God as the first uncaused Being.

In summary it could be claimed that the book *Honest to God*, and the debate it caused, was an important factor in the mid-1960s in opening the doors and the windows of the traditional old-line churches in Britain and America to receiving the new winds of doctrine that had been created in the minds of primarily German theologians. It is to that which these minds produced that we now turn.

RUDOLF BULTMANN

While Barth was the most discussed Continental theologian from the 1930s to the 1950s, Bultmann could claim that honor for the 1960s. I was studying theology in the early 1960s in London University in England, and Bultmann was required reading in the faculty of theology—as he was in virtually every American seminary and university faculty of theology also. Although Barth and Bultmann were allies in common opposition to liberal Protestantism around 1920, they drifted apart later. So much so that Barth published a book in 1952 against Bultmann's theology complaining that in it secular philosophy (from Heidegger) had the prominent position; thus, he (Bultmann) was taking theology back into an Egyptian bondage. (See *Rudolf Bultmann—Ein Versuch ihn zu verstehen* [1952].)

Bultmann was professor of New Testament at Marburg from 1921 until his retirement in 1951. He pioneered the study of the Gospels via the new method of form-criticism; from this he taught that we learn from the Gospels more about the theology of the early Christian church than about Jesus Himself. The value of Matthew, Mark, and Luke as biographies is minimal and negligible. Like Barth, Bultmann rejected the way of Harnack and other liberal Protestants who looked for the real historical Jesus freed from the interpretation placed on him by the early church. Bultmann's theological aim was to interpret Christianity in such a way as to be radically skeptical about the historical value of the Gospels for a life of Jesus, yet continue to believe in the essential message of the New Testament. That is, he held that there is a word of God addressed to man here and now via the New Testament. His work as an exegete and interpreter is well seen in his *Theology of the New Testament* (1951 and 1955).

Bultmann is probably best known for his view that the history of Jesus was quickly turned into a myth and it is this myth that we get in the Gospels. That is, we hear of a divine, pre-existent being who came to earth, who was opposed by Satan and demons, and who made atonement for the sins of the world by His blood. Then He rose from the dead and ascended into heaven, from where He would shortly return surrounded by angels to inaugurate a new age. Bultmann was sure that no modern man living with all the benefits of science and technology could believe in demons and bodily resurrection. However, he was also sure that hidden within what he called the mythology of the New Testament was God's word addressed to man. That word, he believed, has to be released through the process of demythologization, which was hermeneutics, a method of exegesis and interpretation. (The primary source for Bultmann's proposal and the ensuing controversy is a series entitled *Kerygma und Mythos*, edited by Hans-Werner Bartsch and published in five volumes between 1948 and 1955 in Hamburg.

Part of this material was published in English as *Kerygma and Myth* in 1961.)

Bultmann first formulated his program of demythologization in an address to the members of the Confessing Church in Germany. They were all faced at that time with the massive challenge of German National Socialism with its mythological and ideological program. Bultmann wanted to present the Gospel of the transcendent God without mythology. He judged that the key to the hermeneutics was the concept of existence: what is the truth about human existence? Man, unlike the animals, not only exists but also has some understanding of his existence. In the philosophy of Martin Heidegger, Bultmann found an exposition of human existence that he believed gave him the key to unlock for modern man the word of God in the Bible for all men. So he was able to interpret in modern, existential terms what he believed was the essential message of the apostles concerning the purpose and meaning of human existence. And he did this without reference to heaven and hell, Satan and demons, resurrection and second coming.

In a letter that he wrote to the Sheffield Industrial Mission in England, Bultmann stated his understanding of the gospel:

> By nature men live by their own will and want to achieve their security by their own power. That is what the NT calls sin. For the basic sin is not the breaking of moral commandments (this follows from the basic sin) but man's self-will and his intention of trying to live by his own wisdom and power. Need for acceptance also belongs to the life of man, and by nature man tries to satisfy this need for acceptance through his own power.
>
> The grace of God is grace for the sinner. The kerygma tells the natural man (which we all are) that he can only find his security if he lets go his self-security and that he can only find acceptance if he lets it be given by God in the knowledge that without God he is nothing. The grace of God releases him from all feverish searching for security and from all resentments and from the complexes which grow out of an unsatisfied need for acceptance.

He proceeded to insist that the kerygma requires the surrender of self-will and self-security as well as trust in the grace of God, which is the kerygma of the cross (*The Honest to God Debate*, 138).

Obviously Bultmann's attraction to many people was that he appeared to be retaining the faith in a truly modern way. However, the question remains as to whether the process of demythologization (which he never was able to perfect) means in practice a total reductionism (as Peter Berger believed it did—see chapter six). However, in the 1960s such demythologization was a popular, even if not fully understood, method of theology.

PAUL TILLICH

Tillich was born in Germany in 1886 and, in the midst of a successful academic career as a philosopher, left there in 1933 in order to escape imprisonment by the Nazi government. He had to learn English, but he soon established himself as a leading philosophical theologian while he taught at Union Theological Seminary in New York. He retired in 1955. Then, with his appointment as university professor at Harvard, he was able to lecture on whatever subjects he chose and did so to large and enthusiastic audiences. His influence has been both direct and indirect. Certainly his theological method of correlation was influential in the 1950s and remains influential among theologians of the 1990s; further, through his popular addresses and sermons (as well as through those who, like John Robinson, used his ideas), Tillich's way of speaking about God and Jesus Christ in terms of "Being" has entered into the ordinary discourse as well as into the liturgical texts of the old-line denominations.

Thus, though he died in 1965 he was, as far as the general public and the churchgoers were concerned, at the height of his influence in the late 1950s and the early 1960s. In fact, on March 16, 1959 he appeared on the cover of *Time* magazine. He was a man of many dimensions who had been a chaplain in the First World War, who had espoused Christian socialism, who enjoyed the benefits of capitalism, who was considered a wonderful Christian even though he rarely attended church worship, and whose public lectures and published writings have proved seminal for all kinds of theological movements since the 1950s.

Tillich himself saw his intellectual work primarily in terms of the interpretation of religious symbols in such a way that secular man could understand and be moved by them. He had little patience with theologies that attempted to throw a message at people like a stone (he had neo-orthodoxy in mind), without taking into account where people were and what their human concerns were. At a popular level, Tillich made his hearers and readers feel important because he took their existential situation and questions so seriously.

For Tillich, philosophy was indispensable because through philosophy the theologian was able to formulate precisely the serious questions being asked by people in order to answer them from the Christian revelation. In particular, he believed that existentialist ontology (the analysis of those structures of being encountered by people as they faced reality in and around themselves) was indispensable. For this ontology he looked not only to Heidegger and Sartre in Europe but back to Plato, Augustine, and German idealist philosophers. How he saw philosophy's serving theology is clearly set out in his *Biblical Religion and the Search for Ultimate Reality* (1955). This appeared between the first (1951) and the second (1957) volumes of his *Systematic Theology*.

Since Tillich wanted to be faithful to the historic Christian message as well as speak to modern, secular man in terms that made sense to him, he devised and employed a method of correlation. To correlate is to bring two things into mutual relation (to co-relate), and so Tillich meant that he would explain the contents of the Christian faith through existential questions and through theological answers in mutual interdependence. So, through the insights of secular philosophy he formulated the existential questions being asked in a secular age, and through biblical and theological study he pointed to the answers within the Christian faith. He criticized neo-orthodoxy for giving answers to questions that people were not asking. But he also criticized the old liberal theology he had known in Germany as a student because it was one sided—"everything was said by man, nothing to man." He himself has been criticized on various grounds, not least for seemingly allowing secular philosophical analysis too much influence in the study of man and his existential questions. Certainly he saw human beings as always in tension and in anxiety, threatened by nonbeing, yet finding courage and wholeness and (as the title of one of his popular books indicated) finding "a courage to be" in God, Being-Itself.

When we turn to his exposition of the Christian faith, we find that it is also expressed in philosophical terminology. He rejected talk of God as the supreme or ultimate or first Being and spoke instead of God in terms of Being. In fact, he deliberately tried to distance himself from traditional talk about God as found in both the Protestant and Catholic traditions. So he wrote: "God does not exist. He is Being itself beyond essence and existence. Therefore to argue that God exists is to deny him" (*Systematic Theology*, 1:205). That is, God as the supreme Being, the Final Cause, and the Ultimate One does not exist, for God is Being, or Being-Itself, or the infinite power of Being. In his popular sermons he spoke of "God above God," intending to say that the God who is Being-Itself is much superior to the God of traditional theism, who is a finite God because He is presented as personal and as a being. Yet he explained that belief in a personal God, which he encouraged, is not belief in a supremely infinite Person. It means that Being-Itself is the ground of everything personal and contains and carries within Itself the ontological power of personality.

Tillich denied that he was a pantheist, equating the essence of the world with God. He maintained that God as God is absolute and infinite, unconditioned and free. Therefore, all ways of speaking about Him except in terms of Being-Itself are symbolic. The word Tillich used in the third volume of his *Systematic Theology* to describe his view of the relationship of God and the world was panentheism (421-22). That is, while God and the world are not identical, they are inextricably united. The world is in God without being God. Put another way, everything finite (natural, social, and personal) participates in Being-Itself. At the same time, God as the power of Being transcends every being and the totality of beings (the world). So, what precisely he meant by the transcendence and the immanence of God is far from clear.

But what of Jesus Christ? For Tillich, He was certainly not God made man. Rather, He was supremely man, who in and through His humanity revealed a new order of being. In the Christ the unity of Being-Itself and humanity was restored, and thus the Christ is "New Being." What occurred in Jesus Christ is what is needful for all human beings—true union with Being-Itself. So the Christian symbol of Christ is the symbol of New Being appearing under the conditions of existence and yet conquering and bridging the gap between essence and existence. Tillich wrote:

> The New Being has appeared in a personal life, and for humanity it could not have appeared in any other way; for the potentialities of being are completely actual in personal life alone. Only a person, within our experience, is a fully developed self, confronting a world to which it belongs at the same time. Only in a person are the polarities of being complete. Only a person is completely individualized, and for just this reason he is able to participate without limits in his world. Only a person has an unlimited power of self-transcendence, and for just this reason he has the complete structure, the structure of rationality. Only a person has freedom, including all its characteristics, and for this reason he alone has destiny. Only the person is finite freedom, which gives him the power of contradicting himself and returning to himself. Of no other being can all this be said. And only in such a being can the New Being appear. Only where existence is most rad-

> ically existence—in him who is finite freedom—can existence
> be conquered. (*Systematic Theology*, 2:121)

So for Tillich it is the case that "in all its concrete details the biblical picture of Jesus as the Christ confirms his character as the
bearer of the New Being or as the one in whom the conflict
between the essential unity of God and man and man's existential
estrangement is overcome" (ibid., 131). The paradoxical character
of the being of Jesus as the Christ consists in the fact that although
he has only finite freedom within the conditions of space and time,
he is not estranged but is united to the ground of his being.

The New Being in Jesus as the Christ is also the New Being
in the spiritual community that is not to be simply identified as
the historical church with its religion, even though it is closely
related to the churches. The spiritual community is real, uncon-
querably real, but also hidden, invisible, and open to faith alone.
Reflecting on the story of Peter's confession of Jesus as the
Christ at Caesarea Philippi (Matthew 16), Tillich commented
that "as the Christ is not the Christ without those who receive
him as the Christ, so the Spiritual Community is not Spiritual
unless it is founded on New Being as it has appeared in the
Christ" (*Systematic Theology*, 3:149). Apparently Tillich came
to his Christology through soteriology, the experience of salva-
tion/healing. In fact, he called Christology a function of soteriology, for it was for him a function of the experiences of those
who experience healing in the spiritual community that develops after Jesus.

Although Tillich had many admirers and readers, and though
he produced a fascinating and attractive philosophy of religion and
spirituality, the question that one is left with is whether it is genuinely a recognizably Christian theology. Put more simply, did he
really believe in the God and Father of our Lord Jesus Christ?

DIETRICH BONHOEFFER

On April 9, 1945, Bonhoeffer was executed by the Gestapo just
a few days before the Allies arrived to liberate the concentration

camp. "In the almost fifty years that I worked as a physician," said the camp doctor, "I have hardly ever seen a man die so entirely submissive to the will of God" (Eberhard Bethge, *Dietrich Bonhoeffer*, 1970, 830-34). During the 1960s it seemed that Bonhoeffer had a special—maybe unique—word to say to Christians through his *Letters and Papers from Prison* and other books. Certainly some of his expressions and ways of describing the Christian vocation rang bells in people's minds and struck chords in their hearts.

Before his arrest by the Gestapo, Bonhoeffer had been in charge of the illegal seminary in Germany run by the Confessing Church (the church that had separated from the State Church because of that church's support of Hitler). Reflections on the communal life and sense of Christian vocation there lay behind two of his (later) popular books, *The Cost of Discipleship* (1937) and *Life Together* (1939). However, it was the material he wrote in prison and that was edited by his student and friend, Eberhard Bethge, that seemed to speak most clearly to people struggling to make sense of Christianity in modernity.

In *The Cost of Discipleship* he made a vivid contrast between what he called cheap grace and costly grace. In the parishes of Germany, as elsewhere in the 1930s, Christianity was being made easy because forgiveness was being offered without the call to repentance, and absolution was being given without evidence of contrition. Against such a distortion of the faith he advocated a costly grace that recognizes the cost to God of Christ's sacrifice at Calvary and that calls for and expects radical obedience and discipleship in the world.

A series of statements in *Letters and Papers from Prison* became part of the general Christian vocabulary during the 1960s. It was conveniently forgotten (in most cases) that they represented tentative and obscure groping by a man living under the most difficult of conditions. This was because they seemed to describe perfectly what radical minds and voices wanted to say.

Speaking of the autonomy of man in the scientific and technological world and without any special sense of the presence of God, Bonhoeffer referred to it as the world come of age. That is, modern man did not need God as the hypothesis to account for the world as science described it and as he experienced it. He could get on quite well without such a hypothesis.

Bonhoeffer also spoke of a religionless Christianity, by which he meant Christianity separated from the religion of the State Church of Germany that had supported Hitler. Also, he had in mind that necessary rejection of human religion that his friend, Karl Barth, had so clearly commended in his writings. Then, trying to find ways to speak of the living God that were not contaminated by apostate religion, he spoke, for example, of God as being the Beyond in the midst of our life. Further, seeking to describe the life of true discipleship lived fully in the world with and for Christ he spoke of holy worldliness. By this phrase he rejected the idea of a retreat into a pietistic or ecclesiastical enclave.

Writing in prison on the theme of Christian worldliness and thinking in terms of the Christ who is the Creator and who also was crucified, he said:

> Man is challenged to participate in the sufferings of God at the hands of a godless world. This is the decisive difference between Christianity and all religions. Man's religiosity makes him look in his distress to the power of God in the world; he uses God as a *Deus ex machina*. The Bible however directs him to the powerlessness and suffering of God; only a suffering God can help. To this extent we may say that the process we have described by which the world came of age was an abandonment of a false conception of God, and a clearing of the decks for the God of the Bible, who conquers power and space in the world by his weakness. (*Letters*, 164)

Regrettably, Bonhoeffer was never able to fill out these thoughts and develop a truly systematic theology of the suffering God.

Without the threat of the Nazi regime and in the freedom of America in the 1950s and 1960s, Bonhoeffer's choice expressions lost their original context and were filled—at least in part—with the content of modernity. What Bonhoeffer himself would have made of the way his ideas and phrases were used (e.g., by Bishop John Robinson and the secular theologians) we can never know. All that we do know is that they were used, and used widely, in support of the revolution in thinking about God, Jesus, and Christianity in the 1960s. Certainly the radical theologians to whom we now turn saw themselves as continuing the insights not only of Bonhoeffer but also of another German, Friedrich Gogarten (1887-1967), who had also been close to Barth in the 1920s and had written on the nature of modern secularism (see his *Reality of Faith*, 1959).

FROM CHRISTIAN ATHEISM TO A THEOLOGY OF HOPE

During the first sixties, the theology that attracted the greatest attention in the news media in America was the death-of-God theology. Jesus remained a model for humanity, but the God whom He addressed as Father was gone, said the Christian atheists, who were lost in the process of secularization. This theology represents the internalization of radical doubt within the churches. It is clearly to be found in *The New Essence of Christianity* (1961) by William Hamilton, and also in his much discussed article entitled "Thursday's Child" that appeared in *Theology Today* in January 1964. Speaking specifically of the American (as contrasted with the European) theologian, he wrote:

> He really doesn't believe in God, or that there is a God or that God exists. It is not that he is fashionably against idols or opposed to God as a Being or as part of the world. It is God himself he has trouble with. Can one stand before God in unbelief? In what sense is such a man "before God"? Faith, or trusting God, ought to produce some palpable fruits. The theologian may sometimes see these, but never in himself. Something has happened. At the center of his thoughts and

meditations is a void, a disappearance, an absence. ("Thursday's Child," 487)

He went on to remark that in the past the theologian would distinguish among God, Christendom, Christianity, and church so that a different balance of yes and no could be said of each one. Now he finds himself equally alienated from each of the realities conveyed by the four words and says no to each. Thus, the theologian lives in the present with only love to guide him, love he sees in the life of Jesus.

Thomas Altizer proclaimed that God died when Jesus was born. That is, God as transcendent died, and God as immanent came into being. So in his *Gospel of Christian Atheism* (1966) he claimed that "the radical Christian proclaims that God has actually died in Christ, that this death is both a historical and a cosmic event, and as such, it is a final and irrevocable event, which cannot be reversed by a subsequent religious or cosmic movement" (p. 15). Therefore, the Christian proclaims the God who has totally negated or sacrificed Himself in Christ. Paul van Buren had earlier argued in his *Secular Meaning of the Gospel* (1963) not only that God had died, but also that the very word *God* had no meaning. In fact, God-talk was really talk about man and human life and history.

In 1966 in a book that he wrote with Altizer, Hamilton made it abundantly clear that by the death of God he intended to deny belief in the God posited and described by traditional Christian theism.

> This more than the old protest against natural theology or metaphysics; more than the usual assurance that before the holy God all our language gets broken and diffracted into paradox. It is really that we do not know, do not adore, do not possess, do not believe in God. It is not just that a capacity has dried up within us; we do not take all this as merely a statement about the nature of the world and we try to convince others. God is dead. We are not talking about the absence of the experience of God, but about the experience of the absence of God. (Altizer and Hamilton, 1966, 3)

Both Altizer and Hamilton insisted that only Christians can truly proclaim that God is dead. They both saw themselves as disciples of Jesus, who stood against all dehumanizing and alienating powers (of which the traditional God of theism is one!).

Looking back, it is now easy to see that the Christian atheists went too far; and though they caused a minor sensation in the first sixties, they were soon forgotten as the second sixties arrived. They were so married to the spirit of the first sixties that they found themselves widowers in the second sixties as the mood of America changed. By 1967 people were feeling the need to be able to look forward in hope to better times and to a God who would be there waiting for them.

It was in 1967 that Jürgen Moltmann visited America and began to expound his theology of hope. His book entitled *Theology of Hope*, originally published in German in 1965, became available in English translation in 1967. He announced in the book that

> God is not somewhere in the Beyond, but he is coming and as the coming One he is present. He promises a new world of all-embracing life, of righteousness and truth, and with this promise he calls this world in question—not because to the eye of hope it is as nothing, but because to the eye of hope it is not yet what it has the prospect of being. (164)

Addressing the Harvard Divinity School in 1967 he further explained:

> In a time when God was questioned, the Christian faith saw, in Jesus, God's incarnation. Not the resurrection, but the incarnation; not Easter, but Christmas stood at the center. In a time when man began to regard himself as questionable, faith saw in Jesus true man, the creative archetype of the divine man. Today the future is becoming more and more the pressing question for a mankind that is now able to destroy itself. The Christian faith discovers today in God the power of a future that stems itself against the destruction of the world. The God of the exodus and of the resurrection is the "God of hope" rather than "God above" [he refers to Karl Barth] or "the ground of being" [he refers to Paul Tillich]. He

135

> is in history "the coming God," as the Old Testament
> prophets said, who announces his coming in his promises and
> his lowly Messiah. He is the "absolute future" [he refers to
> Karl Rahner] or, figuratively, the Lord of the future, who
> says, "Behold I make all things new." ("Resurrection as
> Hope," in *Religion, Revolution and the Future* [1969], 60)

Here we note that Moltmann is seeking to preserve the reality
of God as the transcendent One. However, he is locating that
transcendence not with Barth outside space and time in eternity
and infinity, and not with Tillich through space and time as ultimate Being, but in space and time in the future. That is, God
belongs to the absolute future of His yet-to-appear universal,
sovereign reign.

The turn to the future (instead of looking above or below)
was suggested not merely by the reality of social life in a scientific age with the prospect of nuclear war, but was also prompted
by the growing interest in eschatology among students of the
New Testament in the 1950s and 1960s. Together with
Moltmann, the other prominent names associated with the theology of hope were the Germans Wolfhart Pannenberg and
Johannes Metz and the American Carl Braaten. Although the
theology of hope never had a wide following in America (in
contrast to Europe), it became a catalyst for the emergence of
both political and liberation theologies in the 1970s in North
and South America. Meanwhile, both Moltmann and
Pannenberg developed new themes and theologies in their writings in the late 1970s and 1980s.

PROCESS THEOLOGY

If it is the case that both the existential theology of Bultmann
and Tillich and the neo-orthodoxy of Barth represent a conscious response to the shattering of the optimism of liberal
Protestantism through two world wars, then it may be claimed
that the second major force shaping theology in the twentieth
century has been the revolution in the scientific worldview. The
first change came because of the theory of the evolution of

dynamically developing forms of life associated with the name of Charles Darwin and with biology that spread through other sciences into physics, chemistry, psychology, and sociology. The second change came because the theory of relativity associated with the name of Albert Einstein, and the subsequent development of quantum mechanics and field theory, had replaced the world of Newtonian physics. The new physics looked on the subatomic world as a flux of energy and a network of relations.

The influence of these new theories led quite separately to the process philosophy and metaphysics of Alfred North Whitehead and the evolutionary, cosmic vision of Pierre Teilhard de Chardin. Whitehead had been a prominent mathematician in England before he turned his attention in America to producing a metaphysics that harmonized with the new science. This metaphysics has since been used by theologians (e.g., Charles Hartshorne, Bernard E. Meland, Bernard M. Loomer, Daniel Day Williams, Schubert M. Ogden, John Cobb, Walter E. Stokes, and W. Norman Pittenger) to produce what has come to be called process theology. In contrast, Teilhard was a geologist in search of man's prehistory, living in China and the East. From geology he turned to produce his own cosmological-theological vision. As a Roman Catholic, Jesuit priest, however, he was only allowed to publish strictly scientific studies on geology and paleontology. So his theological writings had to wait to appear until after his death in 1955. They appeared first in French and then were quickly translated into other languages. His best known work is *The Phenomenon of Man* (1965).

The central but not the only theme in American process theology has been the doctrine of God and His relationship to the world, for here it most clearly is different from traditional Christian theism. It proceeds on the criticism by Whitehead of three concepts of God found in traditional Christian theism. These are the ruling monarch, in the likeness of Caesar (the King of kings and the Lord of lords), the ruthless moralist of the Hebrew prophets (the holy and righteous Lord), and the unmoved Mover of Aristotle (to whom the traditional arguments for the existence of God point). Furthermore, it builds on what Whitehead called the Galilean origins of Christianity—those tender elements in the world that operate by love as seen in Jesus.

Whitehead also speaks of the dipolar nature of God. That is, He has both a primordial and a consequent nature. In His primordial nature, God is the ground of actuality and is the eternal urge of desire. In His consequent nature, God is actually consequent on the creative advance of the world. That is, the world acts upon God; in fact, the world passes into the consequent nature of God where its values are made available for the ongoing process. So, the love in the world passes into God and floods back from Him into the world. God is the great companion of the world and its fellow sufferer. Together with the world, God is caught up in creative advance into novelty. In classical theism, God as God is not changed in His nature by his relationship with the world as Creator and Savior.

Process theologians thus claim that their doctrine of God truly reflects the suffering, gracious God of Christian revelation and also makes sense in terms of modern understanding of cosmic evolution. They insist that the world—man and human events—makes a difference to God, for the greatest reality in God is not His detachment or powerfulness but His persuasive and receptive love. With this in mind, W. Norman Pittenger, the Episcopalian theologian, wrote:

> Now if the basic dynamic in the cosmos is the energizing of creative love, ceaselessly working to provide opportunity for the actualization of more widely shared good, it is not absurd to think that the event of Jesus Christ is thus *important*. For, as a matter of fact, that event did illuminate the past and make sense of the history of the Jewish people (and through them, of all other seeking for and responding to increasing good); it did, in its initial impact and its continuing movement into the lives of those brought within its ambit, stand out as a striking and notably stimulating moment in history; it did, and it still does, open up new possibilities, opportunities, and also real-

izations and expressions of creative good in man's world. (1971, 211-12)

The event of Jesus Christ is a disclosure of God given not in theory or in speculation but in a concrete, historical human act. As such it also provides not only insight but also stimulus for human existence, which can now be seen as potentially the possibility of responsive action to creative good.

Obviously, process theologians insist that Jesus must be seen as genuinely in and of this world and truly and really a man. He was not an intruder from some other sphere or realm and certainly not a divine visitor to this world. He was the man for God and the man for others. And it is in this man as a personal agent that God could and did work. In the totality of the humanity of Jesus there was an activity of the divine. Thus, "Jesus is the coincidence of God's action or agency and man's responsive action or agency, not in spite of but under the very conditions of genuinely human life—and that, Christians believe, in a degree not elsewhere known in human experience" (ibid., 211). So Jesus is unique not in that He is the eternal Son of God made man, but in that He is the fullest and most wonderful example of a man who expressed God's presence and action in what He was and did.

Teilhard, who was not familiar with Whitehead's philosophy, produced a kind of evolutionary mysticism, with Christ at its origins, center, and goal as the alpha and the omega. He was concerned specifically with the role of Christ in an evolving and convergent universe. He concentrates on the cosmic Christ, who is present throughout the physical universe where He draws all things toward a developing and converging unity. Thus, Teilhard wrote in a piece entitled "My Universe":

> All around us, Christ is physically active in order to control all things. From the ultimate vibration of the atom to the loftiest mystical contemplation; from the lightest breeze that ruffles the air to the broadest currents of life and thought, he ceaselessly animates, without disturbing, all the earth's processes. And in return Christ gains physically from every

one of them. Everything that is good in the universe (that is, everything that goes towards unification through effort) is gathered up by the Incarnate Word as a nourishment that it assimilates, transforms and divinises. In the consciousness of this vast two-way movement, of ascent and descent, by which the development of the Pleroma (that is the bringing of the universe to maturity) is being effected, the believer can find astonishing illumination and strength for the direction and maintenance of his effort. Faith in the universal Christ is exhaustibly fruitful in the moral and mystical fields. (1968, 60)

This teaching on the cosmic or universal Christ proved very attractive in the 1960s and 1970s both to Roman Catholics and Protestants. It had a devotional or spiritual attraction that the more cerebral process theology lacked. Further, it has provided inspiration and substance to modern theologies of nature, of the environment, and of ecology, created in the 1970s and 1980s. In contrast, process theology has also been utilized by the more academically oriented feminist theologians (e.g., Sally MacFague) as a way of developing panentheism (the world is in God and therefore God is appropriately thought of as the mother who births the world and expresses herself in the cycles of nature).

FOR FURTHER READING

Bethge, Eberhard. *Costly Grace: An Introduction to Dietrich Bonhoeffer*. San Francisco: Harper & Row, 1979.

_____. *Dietrich Bonhoeffer*. London: Collins, 1970.

Bonhoeffer, Dietrich. *Letters and Papers from Prison*. New York: Macmillan, 1963.

Bultmann, Rudolf. *Kerygma and Myth*. New York: Harper & Row, 1961.

Cousins, Ewart H., ed. *Process Theology: Basic Writings*. New York: Newman, 1971.

Edwards, David L., ed. *The Honest to God Debate*. Philadelphia: Westminster, 1963.

Ice, Jackson Lee and John J. Carey, eds. *The Death of God Debate*. Philadelphia: Westminster, 1967.

Moltmann, Jürgen. *Theology of Hope*. New York: Harper & Row, 1967.

Pittenger, W. Norman. 1968. *Process Thought and Christian Faith*. New York: Macmillan.

Robinson, John. *Honest to God*. Philadelphia: Westminster, 1963.

Sweet, Leonard I. "The 1960s: The Crises of Liberal Christianity and the Public Emergence of Evangelicalism." In *Evangelicalism and Modern America*. Edited by George Marsden. Grand Rapids, Mich.: Eerdmans, 1984.

Taylor, Mark Kline, ed. *Paul Tillich: Theologian of the Boundaries*. San Francisco: Collins, 1987.

Teilhard de Chardin, Pierre. *The Phenomenon of Man*. New York: Harper, 1959.

Tillich, Paul. *Systematic Theology*. 3 vols. in one. Chicago: University of Chicago Press, 1967.

Special note: From 1964 until 1973 a series of yearly anthologies were published. They contained reprints of what was judged to be those articles and essays that contained significant explorations and directions in theology. See Marty, Martin E. and Dean G. Peerman, eds. *The New Theology*. 10 vols. New York: Macmillan, 1964-73.

APPENDIX: ROMAN CATHOLICISM IN THE 1960s

From 1962 to 1965 the Second Vatican Council met in Rome. In terms of the development of Roman Catholicism, this was a momentous event. While most of the preparatory material for the assembled bishops was finished by 1962 by theologians schooled in the neo-Scholastic method, the documents from the bishops reflected not only a pastoral approach but also, and importantly, what is best called the phenomenological approach. That is, the bishops answered the question: Church, what you do you say of yourself? By so doing, the Council encouraged a philosophical pluralism; not only Thomas Aquinas but other philosophers (e.g., Husserl and Heidegger) could be used by Catholic theologians.

Since Pope John XXIII desired that the Council should relate the church more positively toward the modern world (the famous policy of *aggiornamento*), he urged that the bishops use such language as would communicate their message to people who were not schooled in technical philosophy. By so doing the Council encouraged a positive attitude toward modernity (which was not evident in neo-Scholasticism) and toward pluralism.

The Pope also desired that the Council contribute to Christian unity. The bishops shared this concern; thus, to open possible dialogue with Greek and Russian Orthodox Churches, as well as with the major Protestant churches of Europe, they spoke and wrote in terms that could be appreciated by these so-called separated brethren. A common basis for dialogue was not to be found in neo-Scholasticism but rather in a return to the Scriptures and to the Fathers of the undivided church of the first millennium. By so doing, the Council encouraged biblical studies and historical studies similar to those being pursued in the Protestant faculties of theology in Europe.

Finally, the bishops (of whom about one half were from the Third World) wanted the faith to be stated in ways that would make sense to people outside Western culture. This they did and by so doing encouraged the study of the connection of Christianity to other religions, to diverse cultures, and to people in different economic and social situations.

Whatever the good intentions of the bishops were, the result of their opening the windows of the church to the winds of modernity was the speedy erosion of traditional faith and practice. Neither the Pope nor the bishops were able to control the dismemberment and reconstruction of theology that took place after 1965. This activity, encouraged by a hungry press and willing publishers, occurred as great changes took place in the parishes. Instead of the Latin Mass came the vernacular, simplified Mass, and instead of the organ, guitars were heard. Since 1978 under Pope John Paul, there has been somewhat of a reassertion of traditional authority, but it is of a limited nature. The fact is that Roman Catholic theology is now much like liberal Protestant theology, encompassing a spectrum from neo-Scholasticism through to radical feminism, and there are few effective controls on what Roman Catholic theologians say and write.

We await the results of the reception and use of the long-anticipated new *Universal Catechism of the Catholic Church* (1994) in the parishes. It has been more than four hundred years since a catechism of such authority has appeared. In 1566, as mandated by the Council of Trent, the last universal Roman Catechism (the catechism of Pope Pius V) was published. The present one, which has already proved a best seller in Europe, was seriously delayed in its publication in America until June 1994 because within the ideological divisions of the Catholic Church there was no agreement among the bishops as to how it should be translated (e.g., whether inclusive language be used, and if so how much). Produced by the more conservative elements in the church, the catechism represents an attempt to recover lost theological ground—to go back, as it were, to the Second Vatican Council.

While Vatican II reflected two theological trends—*aggiornamento* (updating) and *ressourcement* (a return to the sources of Bible and Fathers)—the publication of the catechism, with the obvious agreement of the Pope, represents *reaccentramento* (recentering). That is, the contents are meant to balance and include the two trends without submitting to the secularism of modernity. In this achievement, the new catechism contrasts with certain national ones produced soon after Vatican II. They tended to be so zealously modern that they minimized or left out traditional elements of Christian faith. The *Universal Catechism* is divided into four parts—the Apostles' Creed, the Sacraments, the Commandments, and the Lord's Prayer.

Although having a very traditional base and structure, the catechism does nevertheless address modern questions in a modern way without losing the essence of the faith. Time will tell whether or not it succeeds in bringing a more conservative ethos and content back into Western European and American Catholicism and does for the church what Vatican II has failed to do.

Chapter 5

Typology:
Describing Modern
Theology

If we have now arrived at the point where we have some notion of the heredity from which, and the environment in which, modern forms of theology develop, then we are ready to face the problem of how to describe contemporary theologies. This is no easy task, but we must make a valiant effort.

WHO IS GOD?

One way of evaluating any theology is to ask of it, who (or what) is God? We can all agree that this is a reasonable and basic question since theology after all literally means "the study of God." If we do actually ask this question not only of liberal theology but also of all the theologies that have been conceived from it and insist on receiving an answer in plain words, we then could claim—possibly to our surprise—to have a general introduction to the different forms of theism that have attracted Western minds in modern times. We would have discovered that there is no general agreement as to who God is, even among theologians. In fact, some theologians appear not to believe in God!

Perhaps it can be claimed that before modern times most people in Western culture had, generally speaking, the same idea of God, even though their ability to express their belief widely differed. To believe in God meant to believe in a supernatural

Being or eternal Spirit who is other than the world and yet is somehow present in the world. It was to hold that while God is present in and through the world He is not confined by the world, for He is the creator of the world and exists over against it. So the older theologians spoke of the transcendence of God— God above and beyond the world; and of the immanence of God—God present within His creation; and they insisted that logically His transcendence is before His immanence. That is, God was God unto Himself before He made both a spiritual universe with angels to dwell in it and a physical universe with mankind to dwell in it.

Certainly the teaching of the medieval church and then, from the sixteenth century, of the Roman Catholic and Protestant churches was clear concerning who God is, whether the answer was in philosophical or biblical terminology. For example, the first of the Thirty-Nine Articles of the Church of England from the sixteenth century states:

> There is but one living and true God, everlasting, without body, parts or passions; of infinite power, wisdom, or passions; of infinite power, wisdom and goodness; the Maker and Preserver of all things both visible and invisible. And in unity of this Godhead there be three Persons, of one substance, power and eternity; the Father, the Son and the Holy Ghost.

Here God-as-God-is-in-Himself (the transcendence of God) is given priority over God-as-God-is-toward/in-the world (the immanence of God).

Bearing all this in mind, one way to seek to make sense of modern theology from Schleiermacher to the present is to ask how each theologian or each school of theology handles the relationship of transcendence to immanence—as long as there is clarity as to what these terms mean. If, for example, the theology is not historic, classical, Trinitarian theism but rather a form of unitarianism or panentheism (literally, "the world is in God"), then transcendence will not be the same concept for each of the three.

Setting transcendence and immanence as two poles, Stanley

J. Grenz and Roger E. Olson seek to analyze modern theology in relation to them in their recent and valuable book, *Twentieth Century Theology* (1992). Introducing their comprehensive description of twentieth-century theology (which covers both Protestant and Roman Catholic theology as well as everything from classical liberal theology through neo-orthodoxy to modern narrative theology) they write:

> Because the Bible presents God as both beyond and present in the world, theologians in every era are confronted with the challenge of articulating the Christian understanding of the nature of God in a manner that balances, affirms and holds in creative tension the twin truths of the divine transcendence and the divine immanence. A balanced affirmation of both truths facilitates a proper relation between theology and reason or culture. Where such a balance is lacking, serious theological problems readily emerge. Hence an overemphasis on transcendence can lead to a theology that is irrelevant in the cultural context in which it seeks to speak, whereas an overemphasis on immanence can produce a theology held captive to a specific culture. (11-12)

The authors maintain that the theology of the twentieth century offers an interesting case study in the attempt to balance these two aspects of the relation of God to creation. As we noted in chapter two, the dominant theology at the beginning of the century and before the First World War was the optimistic emphasis on divine immanence, with the confidence that God was at work in the world and in human affairs. Grenz and Olson maintain that the theological agenda of this century has been determined to a great degree by the aftermath of that war.

Their method is to expound the emerging and various theologies of this century with respect to the two poles of transcendence and immanence. A possible weakness of this method is that (1) it presupposes that there ought to be a balance between the two poles, and (2) it presupposes that the concepts of transcendence and immanence are constant. In my judgment both suppositions are in question and would benefit from further clarity. This said, *Twentieth Century Theology* is an extremely useful survey of different theologies.

AN ECUMENICAL PROPOSAL

Those who have watched the progress of the discussions by theological commissions of member churches of the ecumenical movement (the World Council of Churches and National Councils of Churches) over the last thirty years have often been surprised by the announcement of agreements in doctrine. Whether it be Anglicans and Roman Catholics, Roman Catholics and Lutherans, or Lutherans and Anglicans, the story has been much the same. Theologians from the separate churches and claiming to hold to the doctrines of their churches have put their signatures to common statements in which doctrinal agreement on such topics as justification, the Lord's Supper, and authority is claimed. In other words, theologians involved in ecumenical dialogue have appeared to be saying two contradictory things—one in their own churches and another in the dialogue with other churches.

Assuming the honesty and goodwill of these theologians, how can such apparent double-mindedness be explained? This is where George A. Lindbeck of Yale University seeks to make a positive contribution in his much-discussed book *The Nature of Doctrine: Religion and Theology in a Postliberal Age* (1984). His proposals have occasioned debate within both academia and the ecumenical movement. (See, for example, the book *Theology and Dialogue: Essays in Conversation with George Lindbeck* [1990], edited by Bruce D. Marshall.) Lindbeck's approach is first to describe the way doctrine has been, and is currently, understood in the churches. Then he proposes a new way of understanding it, claiming that this new way accounts for the theological agreements of those involved in ecumenical dialogue.

As he surveyed the theological scene in the early 1980s Lindbeck believed that the most familiar theological theories of religion and doctrine could be divided into three types. First of all, there is that traditional way of doing theology that emphasizes the cognitive aspects of religion and stresses the ways in which church doctrines function as informative propositions or truth claims about objective realities. He recognized this approach in the classic orthodoxies of all the major Christian traditions, from Roman Catholicism through Russian Orthodoxy to Presbyterianism. It was the approach of those who composed the doctrinal statements of the ecumenical councils of the patristic era, as well as of the Puritans who wrote the Westminster Confession of Faith in 1647. Lindbeck also recognized this approach in a very modern form in the way that recent Anglo-Saxon analytical philosophy emphasizes the cognitive or informational meaningfulness of religious utterances and statements (see, for example, D. Z. Phillips, *Faith and Philosophical Enquiry*, [1979]).

In the second place, there is that way of doing theology that has been in vogue since the early nineteenth century that is based on the experiential-expressive dimension of religion. Here doctrines are interpreted as "noninformative and nondiscursive symbols of inner feelings, attitudes, or existential orientations" (Lindbeck, *The Nature of Doctrine*, 17). Such an approach has characterized liberal theology since Schleiermacher defined religion in terms of a sense and feeling of absolute dependence on that Reality we call God, and since he proceeded to base theological reflection on the reported religious experience of men.

In the third place, there is that hybrid way of doing theology that seeks to combine the first and second options. That is to unite the cognitively propositional with the expressively symbolic approaches in order to get the best of both worlds. Lindbeck found such an approach in the writings of distinguished Roman Catholic theologians—the German Karl Rahner and the French Canadian Bernard Lonergan. (See further the appendix at the end of this chapter.)

In terms of ecumenical discussion, those participants (and they tend to be few in the modern era) who hold to the cognitively propositional approach find it the most difficult to come to any agreements. This is primarily because they cannot see how two sets of different propositions can be said to mean one and the same thing. For example, how can the doctrine of justification by faith in the Lutheran Augsburg Confession of Faith be said to harmonize with the doctrine of justification in the Decrees and Canons of the Council of Trent? Here doctrinal reconciliation seems to mean doctrinal capitulation by one side or the other.

In contrast, those participants who are experiential-expressive symbolists are able to agree on meaning while disagreeing on doctrinal formulations. For them, the truth is that to which the statement or symbol points; it is not contained in propositional form in the theological wording of sentences and paragraphs. Here "the general principle is that insofar as doctrines function as nondiscursive symbols, they are polyvalent in import and therefore subject to changes of meaning or even to the loss of meaningfulness, to what Paul Tillich calls their death" (ibid., 17). Here again doctrinal reconciliation seems to require capitulation either to the meaning proposed by the other side or to a new meaning to which the contrary sets of symbols point.

On first sight, the theories that utilize both cognitive and experiential-expressive perspectives seem to be better fitted to find a way of showing how there can be genuine doctrinal agreement by those who have disagreed or do disagree still. Lindbeck's assessment, however, is that they resort to complicated intellectual gymnastics (and those who have read the more intellectual works of Rahner and Lonergan will understand this claim) and in the end are not convincing.

As a result, Lindbeck stepped into the void in order to propose an understanding of doctrine and theology that makes the intertwining of invariability and variability in matters of faith easier to understand and appreciate. His proposal was for a cultural-linguistic approach with the implied view of church doctrine as regulative, or functioning as a rule. His claim is that a regulative approach has no difficulty in explaining reconciliation without capitulation. He writes:

> Rules, unlike propositions or expressive symbols, retain an invariant meaning under changing conditions of comparability and conflict. For example, the rules "Drive on the left" and "Drive on the right" are unequivocal in meaning and unequivocally opposed, yet both may be binding: one in Britain and one in the United States, or one where traffic is normal, and the other when a collision must be avoided. Thus oppositions between rules can in some instances be resolved, not by altering one or both of them, but by specifying when or where they apply, or by stipulating which of the competing directives takes precedence. (*The Nature of Doctrine*, 18)

So far so good. Then he proceeds to seek to show that when doctrines are understood as rules (which apply here but not there or there but not here) there is no logical problem in understanding how historically opposed positions can (at least in some cases) be reconciled while remaining unchanged in themselves.

This cultural-linguistic approach to religion with a regulative view of doctrine is most closely related to what is now called the Yale theology or narrative theology to which we shall return in chapter six.

THE USE OF TYPOLOGY

Probably the method of presenting and describing contemporary theology that is both the simplest and the most profound is to make use of typology as used in the sociology of knowledge. This was done with great effect by Ernst Troeltsch in his *Social Teaching of the Christian Churches* (1911, 1931).

Bible students are familiar with the word *typology* to refer to those persons, events, and things that pointed from the Old to the New Testament and that prefigured some person or thing revealed in the new covenant and order (the antitype). Thus, David as king is a type of Jesus as the Christ, and the deliverance of the Israelites from Egypt is a type of the deliverance of the new Israel from Satan, sin, and death. Troeltsch, however, developed a different use of the word *typology* for social analysis. He built on its mid-nineteenth-century meaning as pointing both to a perfect example or specimen of something and to a kind, class, or order of things, distinguished by particular characteristics. For Troeltsch typology meant focusing on the structural features of systems of thought as they are abstracted from place, time, and circumstance.

A near-perfect example of this method of typology is supplied by H. Richard Niebuhr in his *Christ and Culture*. Here is his explanation of *type*:

> A type is always something of a construct, even when it has not been constructed prior to long study of many historic individuals and movements. When one returns from the hypothetical scheme to the rich complexity of individual events, it is evident at once that no person or group ever conforms completely to a type. Each historical figure will show characteristics that are more reminiscent of some other family than the one by whose name he has been called, or traits will appear that seem wholly unique and individual. The method of typology, however, though historically inadequate, has the advantage of calling to attention the continuity and significance of the great *motifs* that appear and reappear in the long wrestling of Christians with their enduring problem. Hence also it may help us to gain orientation as we in our own time seek to answer the question of Christ and culture. (43-44)

The enduring problem is, of course, the relation of the faith to culture.

Most typologies are based on known systems of thought rather than on aprioristic constructions. Thus, Niebuhr in proposing such options as "Christ against culture," "the Christ of culture," "Christ above culture," "Christ and culture in paradox," and "Christ the transformer of culture" created these types after the study of many individual theologians. He also had specific theologians and Christian movements in mind for the illustration of each type. Yet he knew, as his book clearly reveals, that this methodology is most successful where there is a limited number of general types and each one is markedly different and sharply delineated from the others. Thus, in his typology there are two poles, the Christ of culture and the Christ against culture, with intermediate positions. He was quick to admit that no single Christian thinker fits wholly into one type, for there are certain aspects of his thinking that burst out and reveal that he is a living being and not merely an intellectual construct. Niebuhr also commended as a suggestive and illuminating use of typology the book *Psychological Types* (1926) by C. J. Jung.

I think it is true to say that nobody trying to make sense of modern theology with its tremendous number of varying expressions can really proceed without some sort of typification or schema. As we noted above, Lindbeck actually was doing this in his description of modern theological method. It is true enough that no typology as such exists in the world of human beings in space and time, for it is always an intellectual construct. A carefully constructed typology (as that of Niebuhr), however, is useful to the extent that it does help the student discriminate among empirically available cases and thereby assists in the process of both explanation and understanding. As long as the student is aware of the rationale behind typology, there is probably no better way for him to approach the tremendous variety and apparent complexity of twentieth-century theology. This said, it must also be emphasized that the typological cannot replace the work of the critical historian who presents and analyzes the work of individual theologians. The typological stands alongside such work.

Perhaps an example of the use of typology by a leading and eminently readable theologian will help to clarify the issue. The Roman Catholic Avery Dulles, S.J. makes use of typology to good effect in his analysis of one major dimension of theology. He studies revelation (i.e., the disclosure of God, His nature, and His will) as presented in modern theology in his book *Models of Revelation* (1985). His five types are (1) revelation as doctrine, (2) revelation as history, (3) revelation as inner experience, (4) revelation as dialectical presence, and (5) revelation as new awareness.

Looking at them briefly will provide both an example and a feel for this method of working. Dulles writes:

> Each of these five typical positions situates the crucial moment of revelation at a different point. For the doctrinal type, the pivotal moment is the formulation of teaching in clear conceptual form. For the historical type, the decisive point is the occurrence of a historical event through which God signifies his intentions. For the experiential type (i.e., the type emphasizing *inner* experience), the crux is an immediate, interior perception of the divine presence. For the dialectical type, the key element is God's utterance of a word charged with divine power. For the awareness type, the decisive moment is the stimulation of the human imagination to restructure experience in the new framework. (*Models of Revelation*, 28)

Like Troeltsch and Niebuhr before him, Dulles insists that his typology does not rest on the assumption that every living or recent theologian can be neatly pigeonholed within one and only one of these five types. If one is to understand hybrid positions, it is best that one first understands the basic types. This said, it is obvious that specific theologians can be seen as belonging primarily but not uniquely to one type.

It may be said that the evangelicals Carl F. H. Henry and J. I. Packer belong to the first type. Here God is seen as an infallible teacher who communicates knowledge by speech and writing. The recipients, as disciples, are to be attentive and faithful to the propositional truth written in Holy Scripture.

It may be claimed that the late G. Ernest Wright, a biblical scholar, and Wolfhart Pannenberg, the German systematic theologian, belong to the second type. Here God is represented as the transcendent agent who causes the revelatory events and by means of them makes signs to His people. The latter are then seen as having the task of discerning and interpreting the signs.

So the Bible contains the signs and the interpretation of them by the people of God who saw and received them.

Looking to Europe, it may be stated that two well-known names from yesterday, the German Wilhelm Herrmann and the English writer on mysticism Evelyn Underhill, belong to the third type. God is viewed as the divine visitor, the guest of the soul, and He communicates by His presence. The prayerful Christian is to be always open to the divine visitation. The Bible is the primary but not the only repository of the records of such experiences.

Again looking to Europe, it may be stated that Karl Barth and Emil Brunner belong to the fourth type. Here, God is the merciful Judge who pronounces an efficacious sentence of condemnation and of pardon. Those who hear and know the power of the Word to convict and to pardon are to be submissive and obedient. The Scriptures are the witness to the self-disclosure of God, whose voice is heard in proclamation from that witness in preaching.

Finally, it may be claimed that the Roman Catholic priest and scientist Pierre Teilhard de Chardin and the American religious educator Gabriel Moran belong to the fifth type. Here God reveals by luring the imagination to construe the world in a new way. Recipients are then to be bold and respond to the call to build a new world. The content of the Bible is one but not the only source of the firing of the imagination. History and nature somehow also become transparent to reveal God's will.

However, a major Catholic theologian such as the late Karl Rahner of Germany does not fit primarily into any one of the types, for he writes at times as though he belongs to type three (the experiential) and at other times to type five (the imaginative). Some even think he also belongs to types one (the propositional) and two (the historical).

As we noted above, Dulles calls his book *Models of Revelation*, not "Types of Revelation." Since the word *model* is much used in modern theology, it will be helpful to note how it is used and what is its relation to type. Dulles explains:

> As an ideal case, the type may be called a model. That is to say, it is a relatively simple, artificially constructed case which is found to be useful and illuminating for dealing with realities that are more complex and differentiated. A theological model might in some ways be compared to a tailor's dummy, which represents a man or a woman of more or less average stature and build, and therefore assists in the manufacture of clothes. But the clothes, when marketed, do not fit as perfectly as if individually tailored. They usually have to be adjusted to the measurements and tastes of particular customers, who may be all judged tall or short, fat or thin insofar as they depart from the normative model. (30)

Therefore, his five types of revelation present five styles that characterize theologians in an approximate but useful way. The typical cases first act as reference points; then each one can be treated as a model by which it is possible to submit a large number of individual theologians to simultaneous consideration.

These five types cannot, of course, be transferred from their connection to one aspect of theology (revelation) to the whole enterprise of theology. If Dulles were to write a book on types of modern theology, he would certainly construct a related yet different set of types to cover the larger field of inquiry. Yet, our looking at his book prepares us to appreciate and to consider the construction of a set of types by writers who do attempt to cover the whole area that is contemporary theology.

THE TYPOLOGY OF DONALD G. BLOESCH

In 1992 there appeared the first volume, *A Theology of Word and Spirit,* of a projected seven-volume set of books on systematic theology by Donald G. Bloesch, a leading evangelical theologian, with the series title Christian Foundations. In the last chapter of the first volume Bloesch presents his own typology of modern theology. This typology is inspired by and developed from that of Niebuhr, but it is carefully adapted to cover expositions of theology rather than the relation of Christianity to human cultures. He presents four types: (1) a theology of *restoration,* (2) a theology of *accommodation,* (3) a theology of *correlation,* and (4) a theology of *confrontation.*

The first type is found throughout the whole church and is the conscious return to a past position in which continuity with the tradition of the church is beyond doubt. In the confusion of the modern Roman Catholic Church in the aftermath of the Second Vatican Council, there is the conscious return to the supposed clarity and stability of, say, the theology of Thomas Aquinas or of the Council of Trent (1545-63). Often this return is accompanied by the desire to see the revival of the Latin Mass.

Likewise, in the face of modernizing trends in liberal Protestantism, there is a conscious return to known theological roots and foundations. There are attempts to recover the theology of the confessions (e.g., the Augsburg for Lutherans and the Westminster for Presbyterians) or the theological exposition of these confessions by leading conservative theologians of earlier times—for example, by the Lutheran Francis Pieper in his *Christian Dogmatics* (1917, 1950-57) and the Presbyterian Charles Hodge, in his *Systematic Theology* (1872-73).

Obviously, this restorationist impulse can be simplistic or sophisticated or somewhere between these points of reference. In terms of Niebuhr's typology, one could claim that it is a theology within the Christ-against-culture category because it is obviously not in sympathy with the modern (cultural) forms of theology and has deliberately chosen to stand over against contemporary theologies. Critics of restorationism, however, claim that it is merely the choosing of yesterday's culture in preference to today's and thus it belongs to the Christ-of-culture category. The point is that to stand against contemporary culture is to adopt a counterculture. In this connection Bloesch cites the view of Emil Brunner (*The Divine-Human Encounter,* 1943, 170) that there is a basic similarity between fundamentalism and liberalism. This is because in differing ways they both marry Christ to a particular cultural expression. Liberalism is wedded to the larger scientific culture, while fundamentalism is joined to a minority, right-wing, or counter, culture.

The second category is at the other end of the pole and arises from Niebuhr's Christ-of-culture category. Accommodationism consciously attempts to present the Christian faith in modern concepts and symbols. It claims that traditional theology is wedded to Greek philosophical terms and concepts and so cannot speak to the modern generation. Liberal theology of the nineteenth century (see chapter two) is a good example of this approach. Here the accommodation was to the scientific theories that were gaining ever-wider acceptance in Europe. Today liberal theology is found in many forms, depending on what, specifically, is the contact point for the accommodation. So there can be accommodation to major social concerns (e.g., feminism, thus feminist theology; ecology, thus environmental theology; and justice, thus political theology). There can also be accommodation to a supposed universal, human experience and global consciousness (e.g., to religious or mystical experience in all religions, leading to a theology of religions). Further, there can be accommodation to a specific modern philosophy—e.g., to existentialism or process philosophy.

Obviously this theology of accommodation is a revision of the Christian message that brings it into harmony with prevailing views, beliefs, and attitudes. Christians in the old-line denominations encounter this general approach regularly in such specifics as the accommodation of church teaching to allow abortion and to entertain modern, secular sexuality (the blessing of homosexual unions and the ordaining of lesbian women and gay men). The accommodation is also present (though veiled in the so-called language of Zion) in the new forms of worship (liturgies) that use inclusive language both for God and for humankind.

The third category, the theology of correlation, is a development of Niebuhr's Christ-above-culture category. The general emphasis here is that Christianity fulfills the deepest yearning and striving of the human race. It perceives and then answers the questions that arise from the human condition in space and time. So while human culture is not set aside or negated, it is nevertheless purified as it is related to Jesus Christ and the revelation and redemption of God in and through Him. Therefore, though a gap between Christ and culture is fully recognized, that gap is seen as bridgeable; and so this form of theology is often in the form of an apologetic theology (as was the case with the late Paul Tillich). Human reason finds its goal and fulfillment in divine revelation because divine grace is seen as directing the human quest of both heart and mind.

In this approach, there is naturally a large place possible for philosophy in terms of being the means by which it is ascertained not only in what are the yearnings, strivings, and questions being asked within a specific culture, but also in what answers are being given to these movements of the human spirit. A good example of this type is supplied by the theology of the ancient catechetical school of Alexandria in the third century (Clement and Origen). Here the best of Greek philosophy was seen as both preparing for Jesus Christ as the Logos of God and also raising and clarifying the questions, which are only truly answered by Christ in His revealing and saving work.

Today the best known proponents of this type of theology are the German Hans Küng and the American David Tracy (both of whom are Roman Catholics), as seen for example in their jointly edited book entitled *Paradigm Change in Theology* (1989) and in Tracy's *Blessed Rage for Order* (1975) and Küng's *Theology for the Third Millennium* (1988).

Finally, we come to the fourth type, favored by Bloesch himself. This is the theology of confrontation, which he relates to Niebuhr's Christ-transforming-culture category. Perhaps it is best to allow Bloesch to describe it himself:

> A theology of confrontation is primarily kerygmatic, not apologetic: its first desire is to make known the claims of the gospel without any desire to bring them in accordance with the preconceived wisdom of the culture. It is a theology of crisis rather than process. It sees humanity as the question and the gospel as the answer. But humanity can see itself as the question only in the light of the answer, which is given in rev-

> elation. . . . A theology of confrontation is ready and willing
> to enter the debates of the modern age, but it is not willing to
> bend its message to the spirit of the age. It utilizes the lan-
> guage of the times without abandoning the biblical language.
> (262-63)

So cultural images and symbols are not annulled; they are made subordinate to the symbols of Scripture and tradition. The primary example in recent times of this type is, of course, Barthian and neo-orthodox theology in its various forms.

In his final comments on these four types, Bloesch points out that the theology of restoration and the theology of correlation tend to converge. The former can become a synthesis of theology and a culture of the past, while the latter is a synthesis of theology and contemporary culture. He also suggests that the four could be reduced to two: a theology of identity (a modified theology of accommodation) and a theology of transformation (a modified theology of confrontation).

THE TYPOLOGY OF PETER BERGER

Niebuhr looked to Ernst Troeltsch for inspiration to develop his typology, while Berger, as is appropriate for a sociologist, looked to Max Weber for inspiration to develop his typology. Since Troeltsch and Weber said much the same about typology, so do Niebuhr and Berger.

Berger's analysis of theology since the Enlightenment led him to suggest that, in the range of possibilities from Christianity identified with culture to Christianity against culture, there are only three basic types—the deductive, the reductive, and the inductive. These intellectual constructs allow us to understand and explain the essence of all forms of contemporary theology, from extreme liberalism to dogmatic fundamentalism. Berger explains the three options in the book to which we have already made repeated reference, *The Heretical Imperative*. In the next chapter I shall develop and extend Berger's three basic types as my attempt to present as simply but as accurately as possible the range and content of modern theologies.

First of all (what we may call the right-hand pole), the *deductive* option is to reassert the authority of a religious tradition in the face of modern secularity. The tradition thus having been restored to the status of a datum, of something given a priori, it is then possible to deduce religious affirmations from it at least more or less as was the norm in premodern times (1979, 61). Obviously, this is similar to the theology of restoration in Bloesch's scheme and to the cognitive propositionalism in Lindbeck's scheme. It can also relate to Bloesch's preferred theology of confrontation. It focuses, however, on what is done when the tradition is restored; deductions are made from it for the present. One reason for the attractiveness of this method is that in the modern world it has "the cognitive advantage of once more providing religious reflection with objective criteria of validity" (Berger, 62).

In the second place (what we may call the left-hand pole), "the *reductive* option is to reinterpret the tradition in terms of modern secularity, which in turn is taken to be a compelling necessity of participating in modern consciousness" (ibid.). In this approach, there is something much more radical than the use of this or that modern intellectual tool (e.g., the historical-critical method in the study of the Bible), for there is an exchange of authorities. The authority of modern thought and/or consciousness is substituted for the authority of the tradition (e.g., the Bible and creeds). Thus, teaching and affirmations derived from the holy tradition are translated into terms acceptable to modern man and permissible within contemporary culture. "The major advantage of this option is that it reduces cognitive dissonance, or seems to do" (ibid.). Again we note that this is similar to Bloesch's accommodationism, where Christ is made the Christ of culture. Finally (at the center of the two poles),

> the *inductive* option is to turn to experience as the ground of all religious affirmations—one's own experience, to whatever extent this is possible, and the experience embodied in a particular range of traditions. This range may be of varying

> breadth—limited minimally to one's own tradition, or
> expanded maximally to include the fullest available record of
> human religious history. (Berger, 63)

The inductive method is here being used with respect to religious traditions (Catholic, Lutheran, Anglican, and so forth) that are understood as bodies of evidence concerning religious experience and the insights deriving from experience. Holding a primary place in the body of evidence is, of course, the Bible, which is a primary record of religious experience as well as the insights based on it. "The advantage of this option is its open-mindedness and the freshness that usually comes from a non-authoritarian approach to questions of truth" (Berger, 63). This position may be said to be parallel to the center of the experiential-expressive approach described by Lindbeck.

Berger himself, a genuine (old-style) liberal Lutheran, commits himself to the inductive option and writes about it with eloquence throughout his religious writings.

As a classical Anglican, who deeply appreciates true, pristine liberalism in politics, and who, following Jonathan Edwards, places genuine Christianity in "the affections of the soul," I am committed nevertheless to a modern use of the deductive option as practiced by the great patristic theologians and the classical Anglican divines (e.g., Richard Hooker and John Pearson). Having nailed my colors to the mast, I shall try to present all three options (with a fourth) in a fair and reasonable way in the next chapter.

I note that in his introductory exposition of theology for students, under the title *Faith Seeking Understanding* (1991), the Princeton theologian Daniel L. Migliore claims that there are only three basic methods of doing theology. There is the Christocentric theology of Karl Barth, a theology of the Word of God (deductive for Berger). Then there is the correlation method or the apologetic theology of Paul Tillich (inductive for Berger). Finally there is the praxis approach of liberation theology (reductive for Berger). Migliore goes primarily with Barth but also pays attention to the other two.

There are several ways of making the three options into five types. For example, one such schema, whose two poles would be the Christian tradition (Bible and creeds) and the modern world, could look like this:

1. *Totally reductive.* The concern here is primarily with the contemporary situation; thus theology is presented either as a secularist theology or a form of philosophy.

2. *Generally reductive.* The concern here is to do justice to the Christian tradition by doing justice to the contemporary cultural situation. Some weight is given to the Christian tradition in contrast to no weight in number one.

3. *Basically inductive.* The concern here is to be wholly aware of the modern cultural situation without in any way making that situation an authority for religion. Theology is based on the study of the experience of God in the Christian Scriptures and tradition.

4. *Generally deductive.* The concern here is to do justice to the contemporary situation by truly doing justice to the Christian tradition. Some weight is given to the contemporary situation in contrast to no weight in number five.

5. *Totally deductive.* The concern here is only with the Christian tradition, and so theology is in a traditionalist form, taking no account of the advance of modern knowledge.

My reader may want to keep this extended scheme in mind as he or she reflects on my exposition of the basic three types.

Another way of presenting these five types is as follows:

1. *Critical of the Christian tradition but uncritical of the contemporary situation.* The theologian looks at the Christian tradition wholly from the mind-set of modern culture and interprets it to fit into this.

2. *Relatively critical of the Christian tradition but uncritical of the contemporary situation.* The theologian works from within the modern mind-set, but he is willing to grant that genuine truth is found in the Christian tradition. Thus, his theology is not a totally secular theology.

3. *Relatively critical of both the Christian tradition and the*

contemporary situation. Here the theologian has a commitment both to the God of Jesus Christ and to the modern experiment (i.e., to the experiment of democracy with its values and culture). He looks at both the Christian tradition and modern culture with a critical eye, seeking to be fair to each.

4. *Relatively critical of the contemporary situation but uncritical of the Christian tradition.* The theologian is committed to conserving the truth of traditional Christianity, but he is desirous to admit insights into his thinking from modern, secularist culture.

5. *Critical of the contemporary situation but uncritical of the Christian tradition.* The theologian looks at modern culture from within the mind-set of a traditional theological system. His mind-set is fixed by the norms of a pre-modern approach to theology and truth; thus he rejects the norms of post-Enlightenment modernity.

Again, my reader may care to keep this scheme in mind as we examine the three basic types in the next chapter.

FURTHER COMMENT ON TYPOLOGY

Some of my readers may be a little confused at this stage by this use of the word *typology.* To them I say: "Be patient. Move on to read the next chapter, in which I explain each of the three basic types along with a fourth." I do not recommend at this stage that they read the rest of this chapter, for they will probably find confusing what comes next—at least at this point in our pilgrimage of understanding. I ask them to bear in mind that in principle our task in introducing modern theology is an exercise chiefly *about* rather than *within* theology (although practically this distinction will not always be clear).

By this stage in our pilgrimage of understanding, other readers may find themselves fascinated by the possibility of conceptual analysis of twentieth-century theology through typology and wanting to know more of its possible use. To these readers I must now admit that the typology I shall use in the next chapter is somewhat basic and unsophisticated. However, I believe that for beginners in the task of understanding modern theology, this simple (though profound) typology is the right one to use.

At the same time, I am aware of, and am personally intrigued by, other, more complex typology. I shall close this chapter with a brief explanation of two such typologies, leaving those who are intrigued by them to read the appropriate books that I cite. The first is that provided by the late Hans W. Frei (1922-88) in his posthumously published *Types of Christian Theology* (1992). He was known as a promoter of what has been called the Yale theology or narrative theology, which has certain affinities with the way Karl Barth used Scripture and did theology.

Frei's proposal of five types represents five intellectual attitudes about two modern descriptions of Christian theology. These two descriptions have been well-known in academia since the Enlightenment and since the foundation of the University of Berlin in 1809, when there was debate concerning these two approaches to theology. In the first approach, Christian theology is an instance of a general class of knowledge; therefore it must be subsumed under such general criteria as intelligibility, coherence, and truth—criteria that are shared by other academic disciplines. Thus, its right to inclusion in the curriculum of an "Enlightenment" university is that it exemplifies these criteria of validity.

In the second approach, Christian theology is an aspect of Christianity and is therefore partly, if not wholly, defined by its relation to the system that constitutes the religion known as Christianity. In number one, Christian theology is defined by philosophical principles and cannot be contemplated except in relation to philosophy, while in number two it is defined by the character of Christianity and has certain relations to anthropology and sociology. Further, because number two is inextricably related to Christianity as a religion, theology is first of all descriptive; it sets forth what have been called the first-order statements made in the course of Christian belief, worship, and practice. First-order statements cover the theological content of the Bible, the liturgy, the Apostles' Creed, and suchlike. Yet, theology in number two is also critical reflection on the logic and content of the first-order statements.

We are now in a position to list the five types and to notice how they relate to the two poles (the two definitions of theology).

1. *Theology only as a philosophical discipline within the university.* Here there is little or no place for the analysis of religious experience within the church. "God" is a metaphysical construct, and to study God is to search for ultimate and universal meaning. As an example of this approach, Frei cites Gordon Kaufman's monograph, *An Essay on Theological Method* (1975).

2. *On the basis of a foundational philosophical scheme, the merging of theology as a philosophical discipline with theology as Christian self-description.* While the scales are tipped in favor of philosophy, a real place is allowed for the internal content of Christianity as a religion. Frei's primary example of this approach is David Tracy's search for a "revisionist, post liberal, and post neo-orthodox theology fit for people in a postmodern situation" as set forth in his book *Blessed Rage for Order* (1975). Tracy's own formulation of the position is as follows: "Contemporary Christian theology is best understood as philosophical reflection on the meanings present in human experience and the meanings present in the Christian tradition" (1975, 34).

3. *Without any supertheory or comprehensive structure for union, the merging of theology as a philosophical discipline and as Christian self-description.* Here there is the commitment to correlation (as in number two above); yet in this case it is correlation in an ad hoc way rather than on a specific foundation. Frei's primary example of this approach is Friedrich Schleiermacher from the nineteenth and Paul Tillich, a close second, from the twentieth century. Both men were clear that theology is an academic discipline and also equally, and independently, Christian self-description within the life of the church.

4. *The practical discipline of Christian self-description governs and limits the general applicability of general criteria in theology.* This is the reverse of number two, and unlike number three, it does not make use of correlation. In this type, Christianity has its own distinctive language. Thus, doctrinal statements are taken as having a status similar to that of grammatical rules implicit in discourse; however, their relation to the broader linguistic context within which they are generated remains only minimally specifiable. Frei's primary example is Karl Barth, for whom theology is neither founded on philosophy, nor is it subject as a systematic enterprise to universal formal criteria. Theology has its own internal rules as to what makes it a science; it arises within the church and is accountable to God for its discourse about God.

5. *Christian theology is exclusively a matter of self-description.* Here external descriptive categories have no bearing on, or relation to, theology at all. This is because theology is, strictly speaking, the grammar of faith, the inside talk of the Christian church. The criteria of what can be said about God are found within, not outside, the Christian tradition. Frei's primary example of this approach is the British philosopher D. Z. Phillips in his *Faith and Philosophical Enquiry* (1979).

It is obvious that Frei's typology is designed primarily to cover *modern* theology—that is, theology since the Enlightenment, and particularly since Kant. The theological writings of the Fathers of the early centuries, the writings of the Reformers of the sixteenth century, and the tomes of the dogmaticians of the seventeenth century will not fit into this scheme.

However, on several occasions in his book Frei places the well-known evangelical writer Carl Henry in type two along with David Tracy and Rudolph Bultmann. Strange company indeed for Carl Henry! The reason Frei does this is simple, and it is worth careful consideration, for it also applies to other evangelicals who share Henry's philosophical approach. Frei maintains that Henry bases his whole theological enterprise on a philosophical foundation that logically precedes his doctrine of the self-revelation of God written in Scripture. "External and internal descriptions of Christianity," says Frei,"are made possible by the same underlying transcendental philosophical structure" (*Types of Christian Theology*, 3). We may also note that Donald Bloesch makes much the same point, not only concerning Henry but also concerning a cluster of "rationalist," evangelical theologians including Gordon Clark, Edward J. Carnell, and Ronald Nash (*Theology of Word and Spirit*, 68).

Frei's typology has been subjected to criticism by Schubert M. Ogden (well known both as a process theologian and a translator and follower of Bultmann). In Ogden's review of *Types of Theology*, he insists that what Frei means by the two basic views of theology is not always clear, and thus his typology is not clear. My reader may care to ponder Ogden's suggestion that a better way is to use the criteria of the adequacy of witness and theology to their content—namely, appropriateness (in its relation to Scripture and tradition) and credibility (in its relation to the contemporary world of experience and reason). Thus, his five types are: (1) theology understood as concerned solely with the credibility of Christian witness; (2) theology understood as concerned primarily with the credibility of Christian witness, but also—and precisely thereby—with its appropriateness; (3) theology understood as concerned equally with the credibility of Christian witness and with its appropriateness; (4) theology understood as concerned primarily with the appropriateness of Christian witness, but also—and precisely thereby—with its credibility; (5) theology understood as concerned solely with the appropriateness of Christian witness.

To ascertain precisely what Ogden means by appropriateness and credibility one needs to read his book *On Theology* (1986), though I give my interpretations forthwith.

By *appropriate* he means that a theological statement or claim is congruent in meaning with the witness of faith itself. For him, the real meaning of the Christian witness of faith is the real meaning of the canonical Scriptures (as studied via modern techniques). So to be appropriate, theology must correspond to and agree with the essential message of Scripture and tradition.

By *credible* he means that it is congruent with the truth disclosed at least implicitly in human existence as such. For him, the ultimate criteria for the truth of any claim must be common human experience and reason.

In addition, Ogden holds that all theological reflection is of necessity tied to a historical, human situation:

> Insofar as theology involves the same human understanding involved in any other kind of critical reflection, it is exactly like everything else human in being thoroughly conditioned both socially and culturally. This means among other things, that theological reflection always and of necessity takes place in some particular, historical situation, in terms of its agenda of problems and of its resources for clarifying and solving them. Consequently, while the demand remains constant that any sound theological claim must be supported by reasons purporting to establish both its appropriateness and its credibility, exactly what this demand requires is also always variable in that it is a function of different historical situations. (1986, 140)

Because this is so, reasons offered in one situation to establish the soundness of a claim may not necessarily be the ones sufficient to do so in another place and time.

For Ogden, as for Frei, theology is a modern enterprise; thus his types are not constructed to make room for what Bloesch calls restorationist theology—e.g., traditional theology from the patristic or Reformation eras. However, Barthianism and neo-orthodoxy would fit into number five in Ogden's typology, while Tillich as the theologian of correlation would fit into number three (where Ogden would also place his friend, the Roman Catholic David Tracy).

FOR FURTHER READING

Berger, Peter L. *The Heretical Imperative: Contemporary Possibilities of Religious Affirmation.* Garden City, N.Y.: Anchor, 1979.

Bloesch, Donald G. *A Theology of Word and Spirit: Authority and Method in Theology.* Downers Grove, Ill.: InterVarsity Press, 1992.

Dulles, Avery, S.J. *Models of Revelation.* Garden City, N.Y.: Image, 1985.

Frei, Hans W. *Types of Christian Theology.* New Haven, Conn.: Yale University Press, 1992.

Grenz, Stanley J. and Roger E. Olson. *Twentieth Century Theology: God and the World in a Transitional Age.* Downers Grove, Ill.: InterVarsity Press, 1992.

Lindbeck, George A. *The Nature of Doctrine: Religion and Theology in a Postliberal Age.* Philadelphia: Westminster, 1984.

Niebuhr, H. Richard. *Christ and Culture.* New York: Harper, 1956.

Ogden, Schubert M. *On Theology.* San Francisco: Harper & Row, 1986.

_____. "Review of Types of Christian Theology." *Modern Theology,* 9, no. 2 (April 1993): 211.

APPENDIX: TYPES OF MODERN ROMAN CATHOLIC THEOLOGY

While the typology of both Frei and Ogden can be used to study modern, post-Vatican II Roman Catholic theology, it will be to our benefit to notice a typology specifically designed to introduce such theology. This typology is propounded by Professor Francis Schüssler Fiorenza of Harvard University and is found in his chapter "Systematic Theology: Task and Methods," in the book that he edited, *Systematic Theology: Roman Catholic Perspectives* (vol. 1, 1991), to which we made reference in the appendix to chapter two. The ideal types that he describes are the transcendental, hermeneutical, analytical, correlational, and liberational. He makes the same point as other writers on typology: "A specific theologian may predominantly follow one approach while at the same time borrowing insights, categories, and methods from other approaches" (Fiorenza, 35). As with Frei and Ogden, so with Fiorenza—his typology does not include the dominant form of theology prior to 1962, the neo-Thomist or neo-Scholastic—theology that is deductive rather than inductive in approach. In fact, his typology could be said to present only empirical (inductive and reductive) theology.

Transcendental Theology

This is particularly but not uniquely associated with the name of the Jesuit Karl Rahner. To understand the meaning of *transcendental* one must know how this key word was used both by Immanuel Kant and by Scholastic philosophy/theology. For the latter it referred to what was applicable to all being. Thus *goodness* is transcendental, for it applies to everything that exists from God, the Creator, through to the smallest part of the material world. In contrast, Kant used the word to refer to the a priori conditions of possible experience. Thus, for him a transcendental analysis is an investigation of the conditions and possibility of knowledge through an analysis of human cognition.

We see in the revision of Neo-Thomism as transcendental theology that the meanings from Kant and Scholasticism are combined. Following Kant, transcendental refers to the subjective conditions of possible knowledge, and following Scholasticism it refers to infinite horizons (but only of human knowledge). However, as used in a theological context, transcendental refers to the conditions of human knowledge of God's revelation. Thus, a theological system is transcendental when it investigates the a priori conditions in man as believer for the knowledge of the truths of the Christian faith. Man made in the image of God always expresses in one way or the other his relation to God, even when he is seemingly denying God. It is this understanding of transcendental that informs Karl Rahner's influential book *Foundations of Christian Faith* (1978). Therefore, the major difference between Thomas Aquinas's method and modern transcendental Thomism is that for the former the starting point and structure are theocentric, while for the latter anthropology is both the starting point and constant reference point.

Hermeneutical Theology

This is particularly associated with David Tracy and his two books *The Analogical Imagination* (1981) and *Plurality and Ambiguity: Hermeneutics, Religion, Hope* (1987). It builds on the work in hermeneutics (the science of interpretation) by Hans-George Gadamer and Paul Ricoeur. It sees theology as the interpretative retrieval of the meaning and truth claims of the Christian classics (not only the Bible but the great books and traditions of the Christian church).

A major difference between transcendental and hermeneutical theology rests in their interpretations of the relation between language and experience. The transcendental approach sees language as expressive. It expresses via creedal and doctrinal formulations interpretations of basic, religious experience. The result is that the expression in words and concepts can change in differing cultural contexts. In contrast, the hermeneutical approach sees language not only as expressive of religious experience but also as constitutive of it. (This is what George Lindbeck argued—as we noted above—in his description of religion as a cultural-linguistic phenomenon.)

Analytical Theology

Here Fiorenza offers two approaches. The first underscores metatheory, specifically epistemology (the science of the method or grounds of knowledge), for method in theology. The second underscores the significance of models and paradigms in theological reflection.

The first approach is identified with Bernard Lonergan, who began his theological method by asking questions relating to the nature of human knowledge and the basic procedures of human cognition. He answered these basic questions by providing an epistemological metatheory. Further, he attempted to show that behind and through theological controversies are more general and perennial philosophical (epistemological) debates. For example, in his description of the development of Christology in the early church, Lonergan sought to show that in the controversies, basic philosophical positions were dormant—e.g., with Tertullian, materialism; with Origen, idealism; and with Athanasius, critical realism (see *The Way to Nicea*, 1976).

In his *Method in Theology* (1972) and other books, Lonergan seeks to show that knowing involves a fourfold structure—the experience of data, the understanding of their meaning, the assessment of their value, and an evaluative decision. Therefore, in theology there is the research (assembling data), interpretation (understanding its meaning), history (judging the implied assertions and data), and dialectic (clarifying the issues and making a decision or taking a stand). This done—and importantly, with a stand having been taken and a religious conversion having taken place—one can move into foundational theology. From there one can move forward into doctrinal, systematic, and practical theology. The concept of conversion is crucial for Lonergan and moves his theology from a metatheory into transcendental theology (and thus come his similarities with Rahner's transcendental method).

We turn now to the second approach. Already we have noted in this chapter the meaning of the use of the word *model* in theology in discussing the study of revelation by Avery Dulles. In fact, his name is specifically associated by Fiorenza with the role of models and paradigms in theology. In particular, Fiorenza points to *Models of the Church* (1974), in which Dulles identifies the models of institution (army, state, school), mystical communion (vine and branches, head and members), sacrament (Baptism and Eucharist), herald (messenger, preacher), and servant (healer, helper). In the last edition he added community of disciples. The value of this kind of treatment of any major area of theology is that it allows people, with a different outlook on the church, the possibility of appreciating one another's viewpoint.

In addition to the analysis of implicit epistemologies in theological systems and the analysis of theologies in terms of models, another way of analysis is that of the use of categories. This last form of analysis is best seen in historical studies that seek to show the basic categories in which specific doctrines were set. For example, with the Fathers who produced the Nicene Creed the major categories were ontological—substance, nature, form, accident, and so on. In contrast, in much modern theology influenced by existentialism, the categories are known as existentials and are based on an analysis of human existence in its temporality. An example of the use of category analysis is in the document from the Congregation for the Doctrine of the Faith entitled *Mysterium Ecclesiae* (1973), written in response to the claims of Hans Küng in his *Infallible* (1971).

Theology by Correlation

Already we have encountered this approach in our description of the theology of Paul Tillich. It originated not with Tillich but with what was known as mediating or mediation theology in German in the mid-nineteenth century. Its aim was to mediate between traditional theology (using a deductive method) and the theology of Schleiermacher (using an inductive method). In modern Roman Catholic theology there are four uses of this approach that are widely followed by modern Catholics.

From Holland, Edward Schillebeeckx (who was an adviser to Vatican II) speaks of a correlation between two sources of theology. One is the tradition of Christian experiences (to which the Bible and the history of the church witness), and the other is present-day experiences (particularly those arising from utilitarian individualism in modern society). The method is most clearly stated in his book about his earlier books—*Interim Report on the Books "Jesus" and "Christ"* (1981).

From Germany, Hans Küng speaks both of critical correlation and critical confrontation. His two sources or poles are the living Jesus (known through historical-critical research) and the present situation (characterized by bureaucratic modernity). Kung's method is expounded in his *Theology for the Third Millennium* (1988).

From a leader of American Christian feminism, Rosemary Radford Ruether, comes the use of what she calls the prophetic principle. She seeks to correlate this principle (which is a supposed biblical word on justice and equality) with oppression in its various forms—classism, racism, and sexism. Her approach is best seen in her *Sexism and God-Talk: Toward a Feminist Theology* (1983).

Again, from another American, David Tracy, comes what he calls a mutually critical correlation. That is, he seeks to establish mutually critical correlation between an interpretation of the Christian tradition and an interpretation of the contemporary situation. In doing this he develops and uses the distinction between criteria of appropriateness to the tradition and criteria of intelligibility to the present situation. His views are similar to those of Schubert Ogden that were noticed above and may be read in his *Analogical Imagination* (1981)—which we made use of in chapter four.

Theologies of Liberation

Liberation theology began with Roman Catholics and was initially a movement in and from South America. It was a theological approach and critique focusing on the political, economic, and ideological causes of social inequality between Latin America and North America and was deeply influenced by the political theology of the German Johann B. Metz (see his *Theology of the World*, 1969).

Latin American liberation theology has now been joined by a cluster of other forms of liberation theology—feminist, Afro-American, and Asian, for example. Fiorenza explains that despite significant differences these modern theologies of liberation have several common features that bind them together as a family. First of all, these theologies begin from an analysis of the social and political situation as they seek to uncover exploitation, alienation, and discrimination. Their starting point is the experience of oppression. From, and within, this position they proceed to look at Scripture and tradition. Thus, secondly, they do not read these primary sources in terms of traditional exegesis and interpretation; rather, they approach them in a critical manner from the point of view of the oppressed. They look for and commend that which supports justice and equality, and they offer a critique of that which supports inequality, patriarchy, and discrimination. Third, as they do this, they seek to recover subjugated and suppressed knowledge—of forgotten symbols, neglected ecclesial practices, and ignored experiences—that supports their cause. Finally, they see their recovery of a true theology as toward a way of life—a genuine praxis that has religious, social, political, and personal dimensions. (We shall return to this general theme in chapter six when dealing with the reductive approach to theology.)

Chapter 6

Four Types of Theology

H ere we shall examine four types of theology that help us to gain a general understanding of the range of contemporary theology from conservative fundamentalism to radical liberationism and feminism. Following Berger in *The Heretical Imperative* (1979), I shall call the first three the deductive, the inductive, and the reductive. To these I shall add the regulative, which is the appropriate word for the cultural-linguistic (or narrative) approach of Lindbeck.

THE DEDUCTIVE APPROACH

"The deductive option," writes Peter Berger, "is to reassert the authority of a religious tradition in the face of modern secularity" (1979, 61). And when the tradition has been restored to "the status of a datum, of something given a priori, it is then possible to deduce religious affirmations from it at least more or less as was the norm before in premodern times" (1979, 62). As a preeminent example of this option he then examines the mature theology of Karl Barth, whom we encountered in chapter two.

Wherever we hear or read such statements as "the Bible says" and "the Word of God states," along with "the church teaches" and "tradition declares," we are most probably encountering theology of the deductive type.

In the revival meeting, when the evangelist holds his black leather Bible in his hand and solemnly urges his hearers with biblical verses to repent and receive Jesus as Savior and Lord, he is making an important assumption. He assumes that the words of Holy Scripture are the very words of the living God, and in this is his claim to speak directly to all who will hear him. They are to stake their life on the Word of God.

On the Lord's Day, when the evangelical pastor at the Southern Baptist Church stands in the pulpit with the open Bible in front of him and preaches his exegetical or exhortatory sermon from a passage of Holy Scripture, he makes an important assumption. And so do his congregants who sit with their Bibles on their laps. They believe that the expounding of the Bible in the power of the Spirit—that is, the making of its message clear and plain—is actually the making available of the Word of God. From it they deduce their present duties of faithfulness and obedience.

If we go into one of the more traditional old-line churches—say, the First Presbyterian Church, it is not unlikely that the pastor will be of the neo-orthodox school who takes preaching (as did Barth, Brunner, and Niebuhr) very seriously. For him it is nothing less than the proclamation of the Word of God (Jesus Christ) from the written words of Scripture that witness to Him, the Word made flesh, and to the Father's revelation, redemption, salvation, and reconciliation in and through Him. Here even though the Bible is studied via the modern historical-critical method, it is nevertheless seen as the witness to the Word of God and the sole means used by God in preaching to make known his Word. The appropriate response to such proclamation is to trust and obey the Father through the Son by the Spirit. The event of preaching is the event of the Word of God.

Our next visit is to an Orthodox church (Greek, Russian, or Antiochene) to attend the Divine Liturgy that includes the preaching of the holy Gospel. Here the emphasis may seem to be solely on ceremony and ritual, but we find that when the priest begins to preach he does so with great conviction. From holy tradition (which for him is the Bible and the understanding of it within the holy mother church), he declares what is the truth and how that truth is to be both believed and obeyed. It is as though one is transported back into the patristic period to hear one of the bishops or priests declaring the mind of God from the sacred Scriptures as that mind has been received through the interpretation of the holy synods and fathers as they were led by the Holy Spirit.

Our final visit is to a Latin Mass in a Roman Catholic Church. The fact that it is in Latin means that it is a traditionalist parish where the faithful have asked for and been granted the right to have the Holy Eucharist in this traditional form. Again there is magnificent ceremony and a great sense of reverence as the service proceeds. After the reading of the Gospel, the priest enters the pulpit and preaches the homily. Treating the words of Scripture with the utmost reverence as coming from the Holy Spirit, he expounds them in the light of the tradition of understanding of the Western, Catholic Church. And he does so in such a way as to leave no doubt that he is preaching the Word of God that is to be received as true, believed, and obeyed.

In both the Greek and the Latin churches the Bible has been taken to be an authoritative collection of authoritative books. Thus, what is read and preached from any of these books is an authoritative word, first from God the Father through the Son and by the Spirit, and second from the church as the bulwark and guardian of the truth. The church deduces what is true from the Bible both for her own children and for the world.

If we were to inquire of the Bible college what texts were used for systematic theology by the class of which the evangelist was a member, there would be no surprises. It would be a book (or books) that claimed to provide a biblical theology (i.e., a theology deduced from the teaching of the Bible) and thus to be an account of the truths revealed by God. An example of a textbook used in such colleges from recent years would be Charles Ryrie's *Basic Theology* (1986).

Further, if we were to visit the seminary (either Southern Baptist or interdenominational) where our conservative evangelical got his Master of Divinity degree, we would also find that his textbook(s) in systematics also claimed to provide a biblical theology—that is, a theology that is both faithful to the teaching of the Bible and also arranged so as to present the truth of God in a rational form for today. Examples of textbooks used in evangelical seminaries would include Millard J. Erickson's *Christian Theology* (1986) and Carl Henry's magnum opus *God, Revelation and Authority* (1979-83).

In contrast, we would discover that the texts used at the seminary where neo-orthodoxy was the major theology were theologies of the Word of God. Apart from the obvious centerpiece of Barth's *Church Dogmatics* we would probably find the writings of Thomas F. Torrance of Scotland (e.g., *The Trinitarian Faith*, 1988) and Hendrikus Berkhof (e.g., *The Christian Faith*, 1986). All these texts presuppose that there is truth revealed by God.

Turning to the orthodox seminary we would find that the primary texts were written a long time ago—e.g., *On the Orthodox Faith* by John of Damascus and the classic theological texts on the Holy Trinity and the person of Christ from the fourth and fifth centuries by such worthies as Athanasius, Basil the Great, and Gregory of Nazianzus. Modern orthodox writers whom they use to help in theological understanding include Nicholas Lossky and John Meyendorff. Where a simple text is required, then such a book as *Orthodox Dogmatic Theology: A Concise Exposition* (1984) is available, written by Michael Pomazansky. However, if pressed, the professors would tell us that the real text for theology is the Divine Liturgy (itself a basically fourth-century composition) because therein are contained all the great truths of our salvation and deification.

Finally, arriving at the Roman Catholic seminary that trained priests for the traditional rite, we would find that regardless of the modern texts that students used, they first gained their theology from two sources—the *Summa Theologiae* of Thomas

Aquinas and the collection of the teaching of the Councils of the Church known as *Denzinger*. Amongst the modern (traditional) texts would be the writings of the neo-Scholastic theologians of pre-Vatican II vintage.

One important way in which these examples of a deductive type of theology clearly reveal that they are deductive (not inductive or reductive) is in their commitment to the doctrine or dogma of the Holy Trinity and the placing of this at a pivotal or central point in their system of doctrine. The teaching that God truly as God is actually One in Three and Three in One is a deduction made from Holy Scripture by the early church (and confirmed by the church in later times). From the content of the truth of the revelation of the Father through the Son and by the Holy Spirit, written in Scripture, the classic statement of this dogma is made in the Nicene Creed as it was approved by the Council of Constantinople in 381.

Traditional Orthodox, Roman Catholic, and Protestant (evangelical and neo-orthodox) writers all state that they hold firmly to the doctrine of the Holy Trinity. This does not mean that they all precisely agree in their expositions of it. Nevertheless, they all agree that it is a revealed truth that does give us insight and understanding (available nowhere else) concerning God-as-God-is-within-and-unto-Himself in His eternity. Those evangelical writers who do not place any high premium on the teaching of the early church seek to prove the doctrine of the Trinity solely from the propositional truths (true statements) concerning the relation between the Father and the Son and the Holy Spirit found in the New Testament. Those who belong to churches where tradition is taken seriously seek to show that the dogma set forth by the church in the Nicene Creed is truly a faithful deduction from the various strands of revealed teaching concerning the Father, the Son, and the Holy Spirit found in Scripture.

The Greek and Latin Fathers, followed by the medieval Scholastics and the Protestant Reformers, believed that by the self-revelation of the Father in and through His only-begotten

Son, Jesus Christ, our Lord and Savior, the church is led into genuine knowledge of God. So the church is able to speak with great reverence and awe both of God-as-God-is-in-Himself and of God-as-God-is-toward-us. It is because of who God is in Himself that He is truly the God of our salvation.

So the Greek Fathers spoke of God the Father, and of the only-begotten Son of the Father (begotten before all ages) as sharing the same Deity or Godhead as the Father. In addition, they spoke of the Holy Spirit, breathed out by the Father through the Son, as also sharing one and the same Deity and Godhead as the Father and the Son. Accordingly, there are three persons and one Godhead. For them, as for the writers of the New Testament, God (*theos*) normally meant "the Father." They spoke of the association of the Father with the Son and the Spirit within the Godhead and in eternity. But they also spoke much more (as does the New Testament) of the relations of the three persons with the world and with the human race in and through creation, providence, redemption, salvation, and deification. Here again there is the priority of the Father who creates the universe through the Son, who sends the Son to be incarnate of the Virgin Mary (the *theotokos*), and who sends the Spirit in the name of the Son into the church and the world.

In contrast, the Latin Fathers (led by Augustine of Hippo in his *On the Trinity*) spoke of the one God (the Godhead) of three persons—the Father, the Son, and the Holy Spirit. Instead of thinking first of the Father, their first thought when thinking of God in eternity was of that Godhead or Deity that all three persons share. Consequently, they spoke of the One God eternally existing as the blessed Trinity in ordered relations in eternity. Their doctrine is most easily read in the creed that is called the Athanasian Creed or, in Latin, the *Quicunque Vult*. Because they worked from the one to the three, they were obliged logically to add to the Nicene Creed the extra words concerning the procession of the Holy Spirit; not only does he proceed from the Father but also "and from the Son" (*filioque*). However, following the New Testament, their major teaching on the blessed Trinity was of the relation of God to the world as its creator, sustainer, redeemer, and judge. In this teaching, the priority of the Father was more clearly seen; it is the Father who so loved the world that He gave His only-begotten Son to become flesh of our flesh and provide a sacrifice for our sins. Indeed, it is the Father who sends the Spirit in the name of the Son to make effective the redeeming work of the Son in the lives of humanity.

Conservative evangelicals have in the main, like Roman Catholics, followed the Western exposition of the doctrine as provided in the Athanasian Creed and in the confessions of faith from the Protestant Reformation. Barth and his followers have proceeded in a related way, insisting that God as He is in His revelation to us is truly identical with how He is in and unto Himself. At the very center of Barth's *Church Dogmatics* is the dogma of the Holy Trinity. If such theology can be called deductive, it can also be called a theology from above (in contrast to a theology from below—the inductive approach).

Finally, the use of the deductive method, of taking propositions from the Bible as premises does not ensure that the results of the deduction are true. There is, of course, more to classic orthodoxy than the use of the deductive method. Not a few major heresies have also been based on the deductive method.

THE INDUCTIVE APPROACH

Induction is arguing from empirical evidence, and this means two things. It means, says Berger, taking "human experience as the starting point of religious reflection, and using the methods of the historian to uncover those human experiences that have become embodied in the various religious traditions" (1979, 63). The great exemplar of this approach is Schleiermacher, whom we noticed in chapter two. His lifelong enterprise was to formulate theology in terms of the experience of faith (a theology from below). Barth, who greatly respected Schleiermacher's intellectual achievement, called this inductive approach "a theology of consciousness." It was the first great example of liberal theology.

Schleiermacher never taught that religious experience was nothing more than human self-consciousness. Rather, he insisted that religious consciousness is in fact consciousness of something so much beyond itself that, explains Berger, "the human subject feels himself to be utterly dependent on that other reality or being at the center of the experience" (1979, 133). So, to start with human consciousness does not mean that you actually end there. At the same time human experience is before all doctrines and dogmas. Of this approach pioneered by Schleiermacher, Berger writes:

> The core of the inductive model is, quite simply, the assertion that a specific type of human experience defines the phenomenon called religion. The experience can be described and analyzed. Any theoretical reflection about religion (including the theoretical enterprise of theology) must begin with religious experience (so that, for theology, the unavoidable procedure is to go from the human to the metahuman, and not in the reverse direction). (1979, 135)

Once this approach has been accepted, Christian theology is not immune from the questions raised by the modern study of history and other empirical sciences. In this light, the Germanic nineteenth-century investigation of the history of Israel, the historical Jesus, the origins of the church, the move by the church into Greco-Roman culture, and many other themes can be seen as required by the inductive approach. To have an accurate knowledge of how it really was, was preliminary to the inductive approach—and, of course, what began in the nineteenth century has continued into the twentieth. To read the famous lectures of Harnack in 1899 on the essence of Christianity (published in English as *What Is Christianity?*, 1901) is to experience the great historian directing his attention to the experiences underlying the theological developments, which he as a historian has traced.

Berger also suggests that a case can be made that

Schleiermacher was also the father of the disciplines of comparative religion and the history of religion (*Religionsgeschichte*). These disciplines have, of course, fed into the study of theology done inductively, for they may be said to provide the datum on which theological reflection works (cf. what was said in chapter one about experience). Perhaps more obviously Schleiermacher is the father (or a father) of that discipline known as the phenomenology of religion associated with such names as Edmund Husserl (1859-38) and Rudolf Otto, whose influential study of religious experience, *The Idea of the Holy* (1923), is often cited by theologians.

Liberal theology, in general, may be said to have followed an inductive method in that it speaks of God from the side of man. That is, it takes the content of Scripture as being a description of religious experience in and among the Jews, Jesus, His apostles, and the early church. It uses this—along with any other religious experience deemed appropriate (from the history of Christianity or from world religions or both)—as the basis for producing theology. In other words, it does not begin by assuming that God has revealed true statements about Himself and His activity and that these are contained in the texts of the Bible. Rather, it assumes that the Bible is the record of religious experience within a changing history and context. At the very least, that history and context first have to be investigated, and then, on the basis of sound information gained by historical, comparative, and phenomenological studies, theological reflection can occur. Usually accompanying this inductive approach to the Bible is an inductive approach to the phenomenon of the human spirit and its religious longings and strivings. At the center of his being, man is seen as searching for the transcendent—even when he is not conscious of any religious quest.

A typical example of a sermon that uses the inductive method would be of the kind heard in my own country and church (the Church of England) over the last ten years leading up to the eventual ordination of women as priests in March 1994. The preacher would begin by referring to the changing situation of women in the modern world—how that apart from being mothers and wives they are also doctors and lawyers and engineers. He would proceed by saying that it is obvious that men and women are equal—different but equal. Therefore, if they are equal, and if the Christian religion is true, then the real Christian teaching must be that they are equal before God and in the church. Accordingly, this is really what the Bible actually teaches—despite appearances to the contrary. Where the apostle Paul seems to be teaching something different (e.g., relations of order in which the male is both first in order and equal in worth and dignity), that which is different to the modern doctrine is attributed to Paul's rabbinical exegesis or to cultural relativism. Such an inductive approach has been followed both by liberals and conservatives. Sermons on other social themes often proceed in a similar way—from experience to principle to discovering that principle in the Bible or the tradition. (See above chapter one, "The Anglican Way in the Process of Changing."

Modern, post-World War II examples of the use of the inductive method by those who seek to be systematic theologians are provided by the late Paul Tillich (whom we briefly studied in chapter four) and Wolfhart Pannenberg, professor of systematic theology in the University of Munich, Germany. From the Roman Catholic side, this method is clearly seen in the work of the Dutch theologian Edward Schillebeeckx, David Tracy, a professor at the University of Chicago, and Hans Küng, professor in Tübingen. A recent study of the theology of Schillebeeckx by a team of his admirers has the revealing title *The Praxis of Christian Experience* (1989). Schillebeeckx, like Tillich, Tracy, and Küng, adopts a method of correlation that seeks to relate to each other the modern world and the God of the Christian tradition.

The inductive approach is also an important ingredient in the methods of theology pursued by the other well-known Catholic theologians, Karl Rahner and Bernard Lonergan. It is closely related to their emphasis on the transcendence of the human spirit, which we noticed above in the appendix of chapter five. Since Lonergan is so clear in his commitment to the inductive (empirical method), it will be helpful to quote from his essay "Theology in Its New Context":

> Theology was a deductive science in the sense that its theses were conclusions to be proven from the premises provided by Scripture and Tradition. It has become an empirical science in the sense that Scripture and Tradition now supply not premises but data. The data has to be viewed in its historical perspective. It has to be interpreted in the light of contemporary techniques and procedures. When before the step from premises to conclusions was brief, simple, and certain, today the steps from data to interpretation are long, arduous, and, at best, probable. (1974, 58)

Lonergan proceeds by insisting that the shift from a deductivist to an empirical approach has come to stay for Roman Catholics. Further, with the shift has come a new vocabulary, new imagery, and new concepts to express its thought. Because of this great shift he notes that at the very beginning Karl Rahner felt the need to issue a *Theological Dictionary* (1965), and Heinrich Fries organized over one hundred experts to collaborate and produce a two-volume *Handbuch theologischer Grundbegriffe* (*Handbook of Theological Terms*, 1962-63).

Then, of course, the inductive approach is necessarily fundamental to those who move from process philosophy into process theology. Here the empirical study of the cosmos via cosmology, anthropology, and other disciplines is taken for granted, and religious experience is interpreted through this framework. Clear examples of this particular form of the inductive method are provided by the varied writings of Schubert Ogden and W. N. Pittenger.

Moving out from those who are systematic theologians to those who write occasionally on Christian theology (in contrast to Old and New Testament studies and exercises in the history of theology) there are, of course, many examples of the use of the inductive method. Take, for example, the book on Jesus Christ entitled, *The Human Face of God* (1973) by John

Robinson, whose earlier book *Honest to God* we noticed in chapter four. Robinson starts from the position that Jesus is a man, a real man, and on this basis shows it is possible to say divine things about Him without removing Him from his human context. A functional or moral unity between the Father and Jesus (the Son) provides, claims Robinson, all that Christology requires to speak of Jesus, the Man, who perfectly reveals God in and through His manhood.

As I indicated in chapter one in the discussion about modern Anglican liturgies, one place where the inductive method has made a major impact is in the theology of the new liturgies of the Protestant denominations. In fact, the inductive method is behind the oft-repeated cry of *lex orandi: lex credendi* (the law of praying is the basis of the law of believing). That is, we search through the new service books and hymn books, and understanding them in the context of the ritual of the worship services, we draw conclusions as to who God is, who Jesus is, and what the Gospel is! The Episcopal Church claims to have done just this with the Catechism or "An Outline of the Faith" that is printed in its 1979 Prayer Book.

The Catechism begins with a section on "Human Nature"—that is, a theology from below. Older catechisms began with God! Its next section is headed "God the Father," but there is nothing about the Father of our Lord Jesus Christ there at all. The whole section, in fact, is basically about God as the creator of the natural order and the freedom of human beings to enjoy the good creation and show respect for human life. Then, in the third section, the covenant (of the Old and New Testaments) is explained not in terms of God's sovereign action in establishing a covenant and then of calling people into it (as the Bible describes), but in terms of the modern social contract, where God is seen merely as taking the initiative. "A covenant is a relationship initiated by God, to which a body of people respond in faith."

When we ask how theologians, who use the inductive approach to establish their doctrine of God, speak of the Trinity, we encounter a very different doctrine than that produced by the deductive approach. Since all the data available to speak of God is truly human data (i.e., descriptions of and reflections on religious experience), there can be no talk of God-as-God-is-in-Himself. All talk of God is based on reflection of what religious experience tells us of the God who is known and encountered in the world, in church worship, and in personal prayer. Since this personal and communal experience consistently points to God's being experienced in a threefold way—in Jesus as Man who manifests God, as the Father who is transcendent, and as the Spirit who is present in, with, and through the created order—then God is said to be a Trinity. It is worth recalling that Schleiermacher dealt with the doctrine of the Trinity in an appendix to his *Christian Faith* (1821). At least this suggests that it is for liberal theology a doctrine of the second rank. Certainly it was so for Tillich, whose doctrine of the Trinity is in fact not teaching about God as God, but rather about the ontological relationship of God and man. It is knowledge of God in terms of man's own ontological structure, as his *Systematic Theology* makes clear (1:241ff.). Another way of putting it is to say that the Trinity is a human symbol of what is in God (as Being-Itself): there is the element of abyss (Father), the element of form (Son), and the unity of the two (Spirit).

Of course, there are many variations in the way this Trinity is described within modern, liberal theology, which has consciously rejected neo-orthodoxy and returned to an inductive approach. These are carefully described and analyzed by William J. Hill, O.P., in *The Three-Personed God* (1982). With respect both to Pannenberg and Moltmann (who are often referred to as teaching a theology of hope), Hill shows how dependent they are on the Hegelian heritage in terms of a philosophy of history and how for them, in contrasting ways, God is the God of the future (and only the God of history in the light of being the God of the future). In Pannenberg's teaching, for example, this God who is Trinity is the Power of the Future operative in the present. This is seen primarily in the resurrection of Jesus from the dead. Yet, this God is not three persons (as in classic theology). He is one person, who posits historically a human person (Jesus of Nazareth) as his other, who also belongs to the essence of his divinity. God (the Father) then acts personally through the human history of that other (Jesus) on others (believers) as the Spirit, bringing them (believers) to full personhood. Pannenberg's theology is now fully accessible to English readers in his *Systematic Theology* (1991).

Moltmann develops his theology of hope, which is the promise of a radically new future that contradicts the present, in a different way. He declares that we must see the Trinity as event, the event of the Cross, and then think of it as history open toward the eschatological. This is presented in his *Trinity and the Kingdom* (1981). Moltmann teaches that God makes Jesus to be His divine Son in delivering Him over to death. In this act of God, God in freedom makes death to be a phenomenon within (not external to) Himself. At the same time, God makes Himself into "Father" in his adoption of Jesus as His Son. The spirit of this sacrificial death then goes out from the (newly constituted) Father and Son and becomes determinate of the future (the climax of the age). Insofar as this "spirit" is distinct from Father and Son and is the spirit of Father and Son, He is the Spirit. Therefore, God becomes three through the Cross; and as such He is the God who will only truly be known in the future.

Both Moltmann and Pannenberg engage in detailed study of the Scriptures and specific exegesis of important texts. Unless one looks at their whole systems, one could think they were adopting the deductive approach. In fact, they are working inductively and so are free to reject the classic formulations of the person of Christ and the Holy Trinity and refashion them in their theology from below.

Returning to the Episcopal Catechism, which was discussed above, we find that it also only knows of the Trinity in terms of God as we experience Him, not in terms of God-as-God-is-in-Himself. In fact, we get this definition: "The Trinity is one God: Father, Son and Holy Spirit." That is, God is triune only in the sense that we experience Him this way. If the Catechism had wished to speak in traditionally orthodox ways, it could have said, for example, "The Trinity is the Father, the Son, the Holy Spirit, three Persons, one God."

THE REDUCTIVE APPROACH

At the opposite end of the spectrum to the deductive approach is the reductive. In general, it is true to say that the orthodox (or neo-orthodox) mind denies the cognitive challenge of secularized, modern consciousness and states the tradition or truth in classic categories from yesterday. In contrast, the radical mind accepts the cognitive challenge of modernity and seeks to make a comprehensive translation of the tradition or truth of yesterday into the categories of modern consciousness. We noticed in our study of the 1960s how this translation was undertaken by various writers, not least by those who, following Nietzsche, proclaimed the death of God (e.g., Thomas Altizer and William Hamilton).

Berger chose Bultmann's method of demythologization as a primary example of the reductive approach (we examined this in chapter four). Mythology is a pattern of thought in which the other-worldly or the supernatural is seen as acting within this world. That is, the empirical world is presented as penetrated or even invaded by forces from outside and beyond it. And not only the world but human beings are seen as being influenced by good and evil spirits. Bultmann saw all this mythology in the New Testament and saw it existing within the ancient cosmology of the three-deck or three-story universe. Further, he asserted that the very content of the Gospel of God concerning Jesus is couched in mythological language.

In a modern world, with a scientific worldview, Christianity is finished—it has no future—unless it can be totally translated into an acceptable modern form. Modern man cannot believe ancient mythology. So Bultmann attempted to present the Gospel in such a way that in its modern form (expressed in existentialist categories) it was the dynamic equivalent of the message of the New Testament (expressed in ancient mythology). He went further than this, however, for he actually demythologized the act of God in Jesus Christ, making that act occur now in the meeting between the proclamation of the Gospel and the response of human faith.

Reflecting on Bultmann's bold program, and calling its result a "model," Berger wrote:

> The model always begins by what purports to be a sure analysis of the modern situation, or more accurately, of the consciousness of modern man. This consciousness, supposedly, is secularized and *ipso facto* incapable of assenting to the traditional definitions of reality. [Therefore] . . . it jumps from the empirical diagnosis that modern consciousness is indeed secularized to the epistemological assumption that this secularity is superior to whatever worldviews (mythological or what-have-you) preceded it. (1979, 111)

It seems not to have occurred to Bultmann that in certain respects modern man may be cognitively inferior to human beings in earlier periods of human civilization.

Since the 1960s there has been an explosion of reductive theologies, or theologies that combine the inductive with the reductive approach. Much (but not all) of what is called political, liberationist, black, and feminist theology is reductive. That is, the aim is to translate biblical categories and teaching into modern categories and teaching and thereby to serve a fully modern, secular, political agenda. It is assumed that what is being desired (a new society, a just order, equality of the sexes, decolonization, and so forth) is superior to what has been, and remains, the present state of affairs. As a result, the Bible and the Christian tradition are used highly selectively to provide a model (e.g., exodus, deliverance) that is then translated into a secular model (e.g., social revolution) for modern society.

Black Theology

In the late 1960s there emerged the beginnings of black theology, of which the most articulate spokesman has been James Cone. His book *A Black Theology of Liberation* (1970) followed the earlier *Black Theology and Black Power* (1969). In the latter he announced his general concern:

> The task of black theology is to analyze the black man's condition in the light of God's revelation in Jesus Christ with the purpose of creating a new understanding of black dignity among black people, and providing the necessary soul in that people to destroy white racism. Black theology is primarily a theology of and for black people who share the common belief that racism will be destroyed only when black people decide to say in word and deed to the white racist: "We ain't gonna stand any more of this." The purpose of black theology is to analyze the nature of the Christian faith in such a way that black people can say yes to blackness and no to whiteness and mean it. (1969, 42).

The purpose of black theology, then, is to prepare the minds of blacks for freedom so that they will be ready to give all for it. Further writing by Cone since 1970 has refined his call for liberation.

> But what is the freedom that is the goal? It is freedom primarily in terms of living in this world now. It is to enjoy to the full the social, economic, and educational freedoms enjoyed by white middle-class Americans. Obviously for a people who have been maltreated and despised such freedom is a goal worth desiring and achieving. All fair-minded people can empathize with such hopes. However, theologically speaking, it is not that freedom in the Spirit and in Christ of which the apostle Paul eloquently speaks in the Epistle to the Galatians. It is a freedom within this world, not a freedom in Christ from this world and its sin. (*God of the Oppressed*, 1975, 24)

Black Theology since 1969 has been ethnocentric, concentrating only on one part of the human race. Further, it has elevated black experience of life to the norm and, on this basis, has interpreted the biblical themes of salvation and judgment in socio-political form in service of freedom for blacks. So it has served a purpose of raising the sense of dignity among blacks, but unless theology can be said to be primarily about life in this world and about God as only immanent in the world process, black theology must be judged to be reductionist.

Liberation Theology

Especially from its Latin American context, liberation theology has been a powerful force in the ecumenical movement since the early 1970s. In Latin America it has had and still has some highly educated and articulate spokesmen. They include Gustavo Gutierrez of Peru, Leonardo Boff and Hugo Assmann of Brazil, Jose Miranda of Mexico, Juan Luis Segundo of Uruguay, and John Sobrino of El Salvador. All these are Roman Catholics, but Jose Miguez Bonino of Argentina is a Methodist. Not all that these theologians have written is reductionist, because they mix the inductive with the reductive method. The tendency, however, is to allow their (often Marxian) analysis of the concrete social and political situation of the poor in Latin America to determine their use of the Bible and tradition.

In the early days of the movement, Gutierrez gave an explanation of how and where he was doing his theology:

> In a continent like Latin America ... the main challenge does not come from the unbeliever but from the nonhuman—that is, the human being who is not recognized as such by the prevailing social order. These are the poor and exploited people, the ones who are systematically and legally despoiled of their being human, those who scarcely know what a human being might be. These nonhumans do not call into question our religious world so much as they call into question our economic, social, political and cultural world. Their challenge impels us toward a revolutionary transformation of the very bases of what is now a dehumanizing society. The question, then, is no longer how we are to speak about God in a world come of age; it is rather how to proclaim him Father in a world that is not human and what the implications might be of telling non-

humans that they are children of God. (*Frontiers of Theology
in Latin America*, editor Rosino Gillinin, 1979, x)

Here we are provided with the essential theme or feature of liberation theology. It is to humanize the downtrodden and oppressed peoples by changing the total structures and conditions in which they live their miserable lives. The purpose of theology is not to understand God and His world; it is to change the world with and for God by right theory and appropriate action. Such involvement in a particular situation, with a view to changing it, is what is called praxis.

Thus, liberation theology has been in search not of orthodoxy (correct thinking) but of orthopraxis (the correlation of thought and action). It is participatory rather than detached. Therefore, Gutierrez described his influential *Theology of Liberation: History, Politics and Salvation* (1971) as

> an attempt at reflection, based on the Gospel and the experiences of men and women committed to the process of liberation in the oppressed and exploited land of Latin America. It is a theological reflection born of experience of shared efforts to abolish the current unjust situation and to build a different society, freer and more human. (ix)

Class struggle is thus necessary, and Christians are called to share in the struggle by identifying with the oppressed.

Segundo in *The Liberation of Theology* (1976) insisted that "there is no such thing as Christian theology or a Christian interpretation of the gospel message in the absence of a prior political commitment. Only the latter makes the former possible" (94). Sobrino argued that Jesus was involved in a political and social context similar to that of South America in his *Christology at the Crossroads: A Latin American Approach* (1978). Bonino defended the right of Latin Americans to use Marxist analysis and categories for their action and theology in their political and social context in his *Doing Theology in a Revolutionary Situation* (1975). He claimed that theology

> is not an effort to give a correct understanding of God's attributes or actions but an effort to articulate the action of

> faith, the shape of praxis conceived and realized in obedience. As philosophy in Marx's famous dictum, theology has to stop explaining the world and to start transforming it. Orthopraxis, rather than orthodoxy, becomes the criterion for theology. (81)

Liberation theologians use the Bible as a means to an end—the liberation of people in bondage. Thus the Exodus, the deliverance of the tribes of Israel from Egyptian slavery, is taken as a central paradigm of God's acting in history and as a promise for the oppressed people in today's world. While this theme occurs in the writings of the theologians listed above, it is particularly developed by J. Severino Croatto in his *Exodus: A Hermeneutics of Freedom* (1981) and by Jorge V. Pixley in *On Exodus: A Liberation Perspective* (1987). To the theme of God the Liberator is joined the theme of God who does justice. Croatto, with others, insists that an essential message of the prophets of Israel was that to do justice and to do what is right is truly to know God.

From the New Testament, the message of the kingdom of God in the Gospels provides another major theme of liberation. Boff wrote:

> Initially, Jesus preached neither himself nor the church, but the kingdom of God. The kingdom of God is the realization of a fundamental utopia of the human heart, the total transfiguration of this world, free from all that alienates human beings, free from pain, sin, divisions and death. He came and announced: "The time has come, the kingdom of God is close at hand!" He not only promised this new reality but already began to realize it, showing that it is possible in the world. He therefore did not come to alienate human beings and carry them off to another world. He came to confirm the good news: this sinister world has a final destiny which is good, human and divine. (*Jesus Christ Liberator*, 1978, 49)

An essential point is that Jesus preached a kingdom that looked to a global transformation of the structures of the world.

For those who wish to read an introductory guide to liberation theology as a world-wide phenomenon by a committed

North American supporter, they will find that Robert MacFee Brown's book *Liberation Theology: An Introductory Guide* (1983; reprinted 1992) fits the bill. Here he provides eight comparisons between what he calls the dominant theology and liberation theology.

1. (a) The dominant theology (henceforth DT) responds to the nonbeliever whose faith is threatened by modernity.

(b) Liberation Theology (henceforth LT) responds to the nonperson whose faith is threatened by forces of destruction.

2. (a) DT begins with the world of modernity and remains thought orientated.

(b) LT begins with the world of oppression and becomes action orientated.

3. (a) DT is developed "from above"—from the position of the privileged, the affluent, the bourgeois.

(b) LT is developed "from below"—from the "underside of history," the position of the oppressed, the marginalized, and the exploited.

4. (a) DT is largely written by those with white hands, the "winners."

(b) LT is only beginning to be written and must be articulated by those with dark-skinned, gnarled hands, the "losers."

5. (a) DT focuses attention on a religious world that needs to be reinforced.

(b) LT focuses attention on a political world that needs to be replaced.

6. (a) DT is linked to Western culture, the white race, the male sex, and the bourgeois class.

(b) LT is linked to the wretched of the earth, the marginalized races, despised cultures, and the exploited classes.

7. (a) DT affirms the achievement of culture—individualism, rationalism, capitalism, and the bourgeois spirit.

(b) LT insists that the so-called achievements of culture have been used to exploit the poor.

8. (a) DT wants to work gradually, reforming existing structures by "supervision."

(b) LT demands to work rapidly through liberation
from existing structures by "subversion."

Although this comparison is somewhat of a caricature, it does
convey the self-understanding of those who are supportive of
liberation theology.

One way of understanding Latin American (and other) theologies of liberation is that they do not attempt to say all that
could be said about God, Jesus, the Spirit, the church, and so on.
Rather, they present themselves as a corrective to past theology
by emphasizing and majoring on that which other theologies
have failed to tell. This interpretation has some worth, but it
does not deal with the fact that the thrust of liberation theology
is to reduce spiritual and eschatological categories to socio-
political, economic realities.

Feminist Theology

All agree that the rise and development of feminist theology is
intimately related to the origins and expansion of feminism in
Western society. Contemporary feminism addresses and challenges everything that affects the lives of women. Even as secular feminism is not monochrome but varied, so also is Christian
or religious feminism. This said, it is possible to see a commitment to various basic principles among feminist theologians.

They all appear to teach:

1. That traditional theology—be it orthodox, evangelical, or
liberal—is patriarchal. It has been and still is written by men for
men. It has the quality of maleness both in what it says of God
and what is says of humanity. So a minimal, immediate require-
ment is that inclusive language be adopted by the churches.

2. That traditional theology has ignored or falsely represented women and women's experience. It has conveniently
read the Scriptures with the tradition-wearing spectacles that see
only, or primarily, male reality. It is as though women have only
existed in the shadow of men.

3. That traditional theology has had a major role in shaping

Western culture and has thereby contributed to the subordination of women in both society and church.

4. That women must become clergy and theologians and begin to teach and write from the standpoint of women—that is, women who are not walking in the shadows of men. This means presenting a new and challenging vision of God in female images and of the identity of women as being fully human and reflecting the image of God in their persons.

So feminist theology is in its fullest definition a totally new presentation of religious experience from the standpoint of women.

But where do feminist theologians begin their reflection? Most seem to begin from within women's experience, which may be subdivided into at least three aspects. First of all, there is the experience of living in a woman's body with its specifically female biology and activity—with menstruation, pregnancy, childbirth, breast-feeding, and menopause. Such experience, it is often claimed, places women nearer to the cycles of nature, making them aware of the interconnectedness of the world. (So, to speak not only of mother earth but also of the mother god(dess) is a seemingly obvious development.)

In the second place, there are the socialized reactions to feminine, bodily experience—that is, what the culture teaches or assumes about women as women, and which women (with men) accept and expect. Predictable emotions include the fear of pregnancy among teenagers, the fear of infertility among older women, and the fear of rape among all women. And all this is in the context of the assumption, deeply embedded in Western culture, that the whole worth of a woman is in the bearing and raising of children and of always being a helpmate in a subordinate position to a man. (Knowing how others define women, the feminist theologian is well placed to offer her contrasting definition.)

In the third place, the specifically feminist experience is a response to the socialized experience of women in a man's world. It is feminist because it is specifically from women who are thinking about and reacting to the way they are treated in a man's world. They are questioning all that they have been told about the nature, role, and vocation of women. Women are speaking out against men's dominance of women, against being excluded from their full potential, against being prevented from exploring the potential of their talents and interests, and against not being allowed to make genuine choices.

One of the moderate feminist theologians, Pamela Dickey Young, writes:

> It is on the question of women's experience that there is most agreement in feminist theology. It is our experience of patri-archy, our experience of ourselves and other women as oppressed, that provides the starting point of feminist theol-ogy in women's experience. . . . I see the sexism in the Christian tradition that makes necessary the call for change, the call to take seriously and foster in theology the full humanity of women. (1990, 67-68)

It is significant that two leading feminist theologians, Elisabeth Schüssler Fiorenza and Rosemary Radford Ruether, are both Roman Catholics, even though they do not teach in Roman Catholic institutions. The fact that they enjoy wide support in American Catholicism testifies to the power of the winds of modernity in their church since the 1960s.

Having attended lectures by Schüssler Fiorenza I can testify both to the attractiveness and popularity of her teaching. Her most influential books are *In Memory of Her: A Feminist Theological Reconstruction of Christian Origins* (1983) and *Bread Not Stone: The Challenge of Feminist Biblical Interpretation* (1984). Her approach is clearly reductive. For her, women's experience of oppression is not only the starting point but the norm of her theology. In looking at the Bible she insists that only the "nonsexist and nonandrocentric traditions" within the Bible and only the "nonoppressive" traditions of interpreting the Bible are acceptable to feminist theology. All biblical texts must be tested for their liberating content for women before they can be considered as revelation.

Schüssler Fiorenza has left far behind the Roman Catholic doctrine of the teaching authority, the magisterium, of the pope and bishops. In its place there is a new authority, that of women-church or the *ekklesia* of women. This is the movement and/or community of self-identified women and women-identified men, whose goal is women's religious self-affirmation, power, and liberation from all that which is deemed to be patriarchal alienation, marginalization, and oppression. It is here, in this *ekklesia*, that she insists that there is revelation from God(dess).

Within this community the Bible can be rightly interpreted and shown not to be supportive of patriarchy and the oppression of women. In one of her essays Schüssler Fiorenza writes:

> Feminist theologies introduce a radical shift into all forms of traditional theology insofar as they insist that the central commitment and accountability for feminist theologians is not to *the* church as a male institution but to women in the churches, not to *the* Bible on the whole but to the liberating word of God coming to articulation in the biblical writings. ("Emerging Issues in Feminist Biblical Interpretation," 1984, 35-36)

She also provides her feminist hermeneutics (principles of interpreting the Bible), which is a combination of four types, each of which functions in line with the others. First, she advocates a hermeneutic of suspicion that assumes the patriarchal and androcentric nature of the texts. From this she proceeds to a hermeneutic of proclamation that decides which parts or themes of the Bible can be used or are appropriate within the community of faith today. Then she utilizes a hermeneutic of remembrance that seeks to recover biblical traditions from a feminist perspective—to see behind them and in them what male eyes had missed. Finally, she advocates a hermeneutic of creative actualization by which women can enter into the biblical world through historical imagination, artistic re-creation, and ritual. By this method the surviving intimations and remnants of traditions within the Bible that truly affirmed women (and have been edited by men!) can be recovered and given contemporary expression.

But what of Jesus? He is interpreted to become the man who proclaimed the kingdom of God in which there is true equality for all. Jesus founded a movement that is truly egalitarian and therefore in which there is a full and rightful place for women. What Jesus really intended and what His movement truly was about is not yet realized. It belongs to the future.

Rosemary Radford Ruether is also committed to women-church, as the title of her book *Women-Church: Theology and Practice* (1985) indicates. In fact, since the publication of her book *Sexism and God-Talk* (1983), Radford Ruether has looked to a variety of sources, of which the Bible and Christian tradition are but two, for material to construct a theology of feminist experience. These include heretical writings, the holy books of the religions of the world, and post-Christian philosophies. Her method is eclectic. She knows what she is looking for, and she goes in many directions to search for it. It is because women's experience is not at the center of the Christian Bible that she feels the need to go elsewhere in search of texts that affirm the dignity and equality of women.

Again we ask, but what of Jesus? Radford Ruether strips Jesus of the so-called myths of being the divine Word/Son and Messiah and reduces him to a teacher who is compatible with feminism. In His relationship to God, trust and love are exemplified; and in His relationships with and treatment of women, true humanity is revealed. But to think of Him as bearing and declaring the final revelation of God is mistaken. God is constantly revealing God(dess) through our sisters and brothers.

I have named only three feminist theologians, but there is an increasing group of them. Familiar names include Letty Russell, Sally MacFague, Anne Carr, Elisabeth Moltmann-Wendel, Catherine Mowry Lacugna, Virginia Ramey Mollenkott, Judith Plaskow, Carol Christ, and Patricia Wilson-Kastner. Yet, as with the secular feminist movement, there is not one agreed-on agenda and aim, and maybe there never will be.

THE REGULATIVE (NARRATIVE) APPROACH

To appreciate this approach, which has been expressed in a variety of forms in contemporary Christianity since the 1970s, several basic ideas must be grasped. The first is the viewing of the content of the books of the Bible as being primarily and essentially (yet not completely) narrative or story. It is the narrative of the relation of God to specific peoples—first the Israelites/Jews and then the church of Jesus Christ. This relationship is rooted in historical events and personalities from its beginning in the ancient Near East (Ur of the Chaldees) to its expansion to the ends of the earth. As a narrative, it is also the ongoing story of the checkered but vital relation to God of His adopted, covenant people. At the center of the relation of God to this history and this people is the Son of God, Jesus of Nazareth, the Messiah. The passion narratives (which occupy about a quarter of each of the four Gospels) hold a unique place, providing the key to reading the whole Bible.

The second idea is that each of us, every human being, also has a story—a story that continues and develops every day of his life. We speak of "the story of our lives" and thereby admit a narrative interpretation of personal identity and personal history. To avoid the bane of individualism, this story has to be connected to God's story.

The third idea is that the church, as the community of faith (i.e., the voluntary society of individual persons), also has a story that it tells each time it meets. Although it has its own local and denominational story, this is not the story that it tells and hears. The story that brings people together for worship and fellowship is God's story—the narrative of God's revealing, saving, and reconciling work as told in the Bible. The local church enters into this unique story in its reading of the Bible, in its listening to sermons on Scripture, and in its act of worship recalling the mighty works and words of God. Thus, it is this biblical story that gives meaning and purpose to a community of faith. Not only the congregation with its own corporate, denominational history/narrative, but also each person with his particular, personal history/narrative is joined to the larger, definitive narrative and is thereby provided with meaning and purpose in life.

The fourth idea is that revelation from God occurs as the worshipers enter into and become a part of the narrative of God's gracious activity as told in the Old and New Testaments. In the spirit of worship and in the joining of personal histories to the story of God's saving involvement in human life and history, the stage is thereby set for the horizons of the biblical narrative and the horizons of the worshipers to fuse. Spiritual and moral insight, illumination of mind, a sense of the presence of this God of Abraham, Isaac, and Jacob, a relationship with Jesus, and other expressions of revelation are experienced. Primarily, however, the narrative in words makes possible the disclosure of the One who is the Word, even Jesus Christ.

George Lindbeck proposed that a religion be looked at as "a kind of cultural and/or linguistic framework or medium that shapes the entirety of life and thought" and said that its doctrines (in contradistinction to theological remarks) are best construed as communally authoritative rules of discourse, attitude and action. What this means is explained in his *The Nature of Doctrine* (1984) in a somewhat technical way. Put simply, doctrines are not talk about God but rather talk about the church's talk about God, salvation, and so on. The primary talk is what is heard in worship, essentially from reading the Bible. Doctrines function like the rules of a game, regulating how the game is to be played—how we are to think, speak, and act Christianly.

His general position may also be called "intratextual theology." Instead of translating Scripture into extra-scriptural categories, reality is to be redescribed in terms of the scriptural framework. It is the text (so to speak) that absorbs the world (or my/your world), rather than the world absorbing the text. Too often in the self-assured world of modernity, people have sought to make sense of the Scriptures instead of allowing the

Scriptures to make sense of themselves! Lindbeck's general position is accessible to nonspecialists in his January 1988 lecture, entitled "Scripture, Consensus and Community," given at the Ratzinger Conference on Bible and Church and later published in *Biblical Interpretation in Crisis* (Richard John Neuhaus, ed., 1989).

Looking back to the first days of the Christian church, Lindbeck pointed out that it was not a different canon of Scripture but a distinctive method of reading it that differentiated the church from the synagogue.

> Christians read the Bible they shared with the Jews in the light of their at first orally transmitted stories of the crucified and resurrected Messiah in whose name they prayed and into whom they were incorporated in baptism and eucharist. Jesus was for them the climax and summation of Israel's history. When joined to him even Gentiles became members of the enlarged people of God, citizens of the commonwealth of Israel (Eph. 2:12). Its history became their history and its Bible their Bible. It was not simply a source of precepts and truths, but the interpretative framework for all reality. They used typological and, less fundamentally, allegorical techniques derived from their Jewish and Greek milieux to apply the canonically fixed words to their ever-changing situations. (*Biblical Interpretation in Crisis*, 76-77)

A key sentence here is, "It was not simply a source of precepts and truths, but the *interpretative framework for all reality.*"

With the creation of the enlarged canon (the books of the Old and New Covenants) also came an explicit "rule of faith." This rule (creed) articulated what may be called a basic (but not sophisticated) Christological and Trinitarian reading of the Jewish Bible (in translation, the Greek Septuagint). In fact, a certain way of reading and hearing Scripture accompanied and was inextricably united to the extension of the canon in the early church. This reading was "as a Christ-centered narrationally and typologically unified whole in conformity to the Trinitarian rule of faith" (ibid., 77). Thus, to read the Bible as Scripture was to read it in this way and in this framework and not in another way—e.g., not as Greek epic poetry. And it is this *Christian* way of reading the Bible that Lindbeck wants to recover for the modern churches. Such a reading takes for granted the work of scientific, biblical criticism, but it does not major on it. Rather, it accepts the existence of the one canon of the one Bible and calls on the churches to read that canon.

Lindbeck and his colleague at Yale, Hans Frei, held that in modern times there has been a serious neglect of the narrative meaning of Scripture (see especially Frei, *The Eclipse of Biblical Narrative*, 1974 for details of this).

> In realistic narratives of the biblical type, the identity and character of the personal agents (viz. God and human beings) is enacted by the plotted interaction of intention and circumstance. This is the Bible's chief device for telling its readers about themselves, their world, and their God. Definitions of essence and attributes and descriptions of inner experience, of states of consciousness, can perhaps be sometimes inferred from the biblical materials, but if these inferences are primarily relied upon, much of what the Bible communicates about God and human beings is lost. (Ibid., 78)

That is, the loss of narrative meaning, through the sole or excessive use of the deductive or the inductive method, has the effect of weakening the glue that holds the canon together. Also, it makes difficult the typological use of the Bible to shape the present communal and personal identity of Christian people. Further,

> Trinitarian and Christological doctrine lose their function as directives for Bible reading (e.g., Christ is to be understood in the light of the whole Bible and the whole Bible in the light of Christ) and, especially for *sola scriptura* Protestants, become fragile and hermeneutically inoperative deductions from the text. Thus when narrative meaning is neglected, the entire classic interpretative pattern crumbles. (Ibid., 83)

Lindbeck thus emphasized the need to recover the narrative meaning of Scripture in modern churches and with the narrative meaning, the classic interpretation of the sacred text. In this context the reading of Scripture within the community of faith would, he believed, be guided by doctrine (the Holy Trinity and Christology) and also generate doctrine (understood as communally authoritative rules of speech, attitude, and action). So on this basis, doctrine is second-order language, being the result of reflection on the first order. The latter is primary because it is that which is both within the sacred texts and that which is read and heard in corporate worship. Theology is, at best, reflection on the first-order language; it is consideration of the content of the narratives as they bear witness to God, the Savior.

Various theological streams have flowed into that of narrative theology. They include the teaching of H. Richard Niebuhr and Karl Barth on revelation and Scripture and the concept of biblical theology developed by such scholars as G. Ernest Wright. There have also been influences from the study of literature and anthropology. Erich Auerbach's book *Mimesis: The Representation of Reality in Western Literature* (1953) and Clifford Geertz's book *The Interpretation of Cultures* (1973) seem to have been particularly useful to both Lindbeck and Frei.

Exponents of the narrative approach include Stanley Hauerwas, the moral theologian, George Stroup, the systematic theologian, and Geoffrey Wainwright, the liturgical theologian. At least two evangelicals have also sought to utilize this approach—Gabriel Fackre, *The Christian Story* (1984) and Clark Pinnock, *Tracking the Maze* (1990).

It is not only Protestants who have developed narrative theology; Roman Catholics are making use of it, though they prefer to call it by a different name. Avery Dulles replaces the cultural-linguistic of Lindbeck with his own "ecclesial-transformative" and comments:

> In the ecclesial-transformative approach, the primary subject matter of theology is taken to be the saving self-communication of God through the symbolic events and words of Scripture, especially in Jesus Christ as the mediator and fullness of all revelation. A privileged locus for the apprehension of this subject matter is the worship of the Church, in which the biblical and traditional symbols are proclaimed and "re-

presented" in ways that call for active participation (at least in mind and heart) on the part of the congregation. The interplay of symbols in community worship arouses and directs the worshipers' tacit powers of apprehension so as to instill a personal familiarity with the Christian mysteries. (*The Craft of Theology*, 19)

Dulles adds that the symbolic language of primary religious discourse cannot be left behind if the dogmas and theological formulations of Christian faith are to be rightly appreciated. The biblical narrative must be recognized as first-order language.

Therefore, we see that what unites people from very different theological positions in the narrative approach is the commitment to the primacy of the canon as canon and to the first-order language of the Bible itself. It is a way of rendering the doctrines of any denomination to be valid but only valid for that denomination in the sense that they guide or regulate its ways of worship, witness, and morality. Where all agree is (or ought to be) on the centrality of the canon as narrative and as read from a basic Trinitarian perspective (as the early creeds— e.g., the Apostles' Creed—declare).

FOR FURTHER READING

Berger, Peter L. *The Heretical Imperative*. Garden City, N.Y.: Anchor, 1979.

Brown, Robert McAfee. *Liberation Theology: An Introductory Guide*. New edition. Louisville, Ken.: Westminster/John Knox, 1992.

Cone, James H. and Wilmore, Gayraud S. *Black Theology: A Documentary History*. 2 vols. (vol. 1 1966-1979; vol. 2 1980-1992). Maryknoll, N.Y.: Orbis, 1993.

Echols, Alice. *Daring to be Bad: Radical Feminism in America, 1967-1975*. Minneapolis: University of Minnesota Press, 1989.

Ferm, Deane William. *Third World Liberation Theologies: A Reader*. Maryknoll, N.Y.: Orbis, 1986.

Fiorenza, Elisabeth Schüssler. "Emerging Issues in Feminist Biblical Interpretation." In *Christian Feminism: Visions of a New Humanity*. Edited by Judith Weidman. San Francisco: Harper & Row, 1984.

_____. *In Memory of Her: A Feminist Theological Construction of Christian Origins*. New York: Crossroad, 1983.

Frei, Hans W. *Theology and Narrative: Selected Essays*. New York: Oxford University Press, 1993.

Gillinin, Rosino, ed. *Frontiers of Theology in Latin America*. New York: Orbis, 1979.

Hodgson, Peter C., and Robert King, eds. *Christian Theology: An Introduction to Its Tradition and Tasks*. Rev. ed. Philadelphia: Fortress, 1985.

_____. *Readings in Christian Theology*. Philadelphia: Fortress, 1985.

Lacugna, Catherine Mowry, ed. *Freeing Theology: The Essentials of Theology in Feminist Perspective*. San Francisco: Harper, 1993.

Lindbeck, George. "Scripture, Consensus and Community." In *Biblical Interpretation in Crisis*. Edited by Richard John Neuhaus. Grand Rapids, Mich.: Eerdmans, 1989.

McGovern, Arthur F. *Liberation Theology and Its Critics*. Maryknoll, N.Y.: Orbis, 1989.

Marshall, Bruce D., ed. *Theology and Dialogue: Essays in Conversation with George Lindbeck*. South Bend, Ind.: Notre Dame University Press, 1990.

Ruether, Rosemary Radford. *Sexism and God-Talk: Towards a Feminist Theology*. Boston: Beacon, 1983.

Young, Pamela Dickey. *Feminist Theology/Christian Theology: In Search of Method*. Minneapolis: Fortress, 1990.

Epilogue

Evangelical Theology

Most books belonging to the area of systematic theology that claim to be evangelical are best seen (as we noted above) as belonging to the deductive type and approach. However, there are some, as we also noted above, that claim to be of the narrative type.

If we examine the theology implied by the popular books from evangelical presses that are widely read in evangelicalism, then it is not so clear that evangelical theology is primarily of the deductive type. In fact, much of the experientalist-based popular theology is probably nearer to the inductive and reductive types than the deductive. The reason for this seemingly strange judgment is that much evangelicalism has been deeply affected by the ethos and techniques of modernity and hardly recognizes that this has been so and remains so. Thus, while disclaiming modernity (or what is called secular humanism), it actually tends to express it in its general methodology and basic assumptions.

THREE CONSIDERATIONS

American evangelicals have tended to be blind to the effects and dangers of modernity because their own identity is actually tied to modernity. Under the leadership of Charles Finney and other evangelists during what is called "the Second General Awakening," it became acceptable to use humanly engineered *techniques* to cause people to make a decision for Christ. In fact, Finney defined a revival as "the results of the right use of constituted means" (e.g., nightly meetings, mass publicity, the anxious bench, and so on). Instead of truth being uppermost, results were taken as the barometer of truth. Put simply, what works replaced what is true; and what works was seen as what is true. Where a method was "superficially" successful, principles were deduced from it and declared to be true. Here is a kind of pragmatism.

Evangelicals have also been partially blind to modernity because they have mistakenly held that its challenge is only in the area of ideas. They have not reckoned with the fact that ideas do not succeed in history and culture because of their truthfulness but because of their inter-relationship to social processes (as we noted in chapter three). If modernity (as we noted in the preface) is a social reality and a global culture created by capitalism, technology, and information, then it is possible to resist the ideas of modernity and still be caught up in its social processes. It is then the case that one is using uncritically some or all of its features (technology, advertising, telecommunications, and so forth). The medium can so easily become the message.

Evangelicals have hardly realized that modernity is double-edged. It has brought many benefits (e.g., air-conditioning systems and hearing aids for the deaf). At the same time it has also made reality to appear to be that which is new, instant, controllable, measurable, predictable, and marketable. The preaching of the Gospel and the doctrinal, ethical, and spiritual content of the Scriptures are often made to fit into reality as modernity delivers and expresses reality. The truth is thereby squeezed into the receptacle provided by modernity and is in danger of being reduced or changed into something other than what it ought to be.

A TYPOLOGY OF EVANGELICALISM

It has long been recognized by reflective evangelicals that what is called evangelicalism comes in a variety of shapes and forms in modern America.I set out below a typology of twelve forms of modern American evangelicalism. It is based on an unpublished paper by Kevin Offner of the Inter-Varsity Christian Fellowship and, being a typology, probably describes no evangelical group or school precisely. Virtually every evangelical will claim to belong to two or more of the types. This typology, however, covers the general range of possibilities and indicates where the theology is coming from. After careful consideration I decided not to add names of theologians to the typology because certain types have no obvious systematic theology texts.

1. *Reformed* evangelicalism. This claims to be doctrinally in the tradition of Calvin and the Reformed or Presbyterian confessions of faith. It seeks to think Christianly, to transform culture, and to change institutions. The tendency is to emphasize the cerebral and to underplay the experiential in religious practice; thus it encourages a deductive and a propositional theology.

2. *Anabaptist* evangelicalism. This looks to the radical reformers of the Protestant Reformation (called Anabaptists and Mennonites). It is countercultural and pacifist, emphasizing servanthood over against authority. Furthermore, it emphasizes the need for Christian community, and its theological approach is usually that of the inductive type because it makes theological claims on the basis of both scriptural testimony and modern experience.

3. *Neo-orthodox* evangelicalism. Obviously this is much influenced by the teaching of Karl Barth. It makes the distinction between knowing God and knowing about God. As a result, it tends to favor the narrative in contrast to the deductive approach in theology.

4. *Charismatic* evangelicalism. This lives in the expectancy that God is speaking and will speak afresh today and that the

miraculous gifts of the Spirit are present and available in the church today. Personal and community experience of God in terms of His gifts and grace is very much at the center. The theological approach is a mixture of the deductive from scriptural texts and the inductive, based on claimed experiences.

5. *Theonomist* evangelicalism. Tending to be cerebral and with a great emphasis on God's will for the family and country, this emphasizes the permanence of God's unchanging law and is post-millennial in its eschatology. Its theology is very much of the deductive type.

6. *Fundamentalist* evangelicalism. This is self-consciously anti-liberal and tends to see all issues in terms of being right or wrong (there are few gray areas). The seriousness of "external" sins is stressed. It is extremely biblistic, using the Bible more as a glorious quarry or treasury of individual texts to be quoted as necessary rather than as a collection of holy books from different historical periods that are to be read in their totality. Theologically it belongs to the deductive type, even if the range on which the deduction is made is limited.

7. *Dispensationalist* evangelicalism. Tending to be nondenominational and pro-Israel, this reads the Bible through a grid (the system of dispensations) that effectively limits what is regarded as the Word of God for today. There is usually a great emphasis on grace in contrast to works as the way of salvation. It is both reductive and deductive in method, for it reduces that material (the content of Holy Scripture) from which deduction can be made.

8. *Pro-American pietist* evangelicalism. This emphasizes civil religion and Christian country and hopes that the power of politics (in God's providence) will bring change. The political thrust is energized by emphasis on personal piety. Theologically it is generally inductive in theological approach.

9. *Anti-American, anti-pietist* evangelicalism. This claims to speak for freedom over against such phenomena as the sinfulness of capitalism, too many rules and regulations, the right wing in culture/politics, and rigid fundamentalism in religion. Its theological approach is generally inductive.

10. *Therapeutic* evangelicalism. This emphasizes inner healing, sees sin in terms of sickness and dysfunctionality, and encourages self-knowledge through introspection. The Bible is used as a support base for psychological theories. Theologically it can be either inductive (creating doctrine from human experience) or reductive (reducing doctrine to psychological theory) or both.

11. *Social-action* evangelicalism. This is much like the older liberal Protestantism where there was an emphasis on caring for the poor, teaching on physical-spiritual unity, and the claim that actions speak louder than words. In its modern form it has also learned from modern liberation theology. Thus theologically it can be a mixture of inductive (i.e., an empirical analysis of society) and reductive (i.e., meeting the needs of the poor) approaches.

12. *Liturgical-sacramental* evangelicalism. This looks to the tradition of worship and theology of the period between the apostles and the Middle Ages. It is favorably disposed to the better aspects of modern Roman Catholicism and Eastern Orthodoxy. It rejects individualism and emphasizes the corporate. In addition, it is ready to speak of the "real presence" of Christ in the Sacrament of Holy Communion and also of baptismal regeneration. The theological method is both inductive (collecting and taking tradition in its various forms seriously) and deductive (deducing doctrine from Scripture and tradition).

Offner makes the point that of all these, only the last form of evangelicalism is self-consciously Trinitarian. Obviously the reason for this is that in the ancient liturgies from the patristic period (both the Eastern and Western rites) there is a very clear Trinitarian confession and structure to faith and worship— "Glory be to the Father, and to the Son and to the Holy Spirit, both now and always, even unto the ages of ages, Amen."

CONTEMPORARY CHALLENGES TO EVANGELICAL ORTHODOXY

The title of this book claims both that the old liberal theology is dead and gone, and that this fact presents challenges to evangelical theologians. It is appropriate to end the book with a few comments on these challenges.

In the face of a variety of doctrines of God, the first challenge is to remain wholly faithful to the biblical doctrine of God as the trnscendent, holy One who is the Father, the Son, and the Holy Spirit. In the face of modern forms of modalism, deism, panentheism, and pantheism there is a great need to state with clarity and reverence the nature of the true, living God as the Blessed, Holy and Undivided Trinity. The Church requires classical Trinitarian Theism.

In the context of many different presentations of the identity of Jesus, the second challenge is to be totally faithful to the biblical doctrine of Jesus as the Christ, the Incarnate Word and Son, who for us and for our salvation became man, died upon the cross, rose from the dead, ascended into heaven, and there reigns as the Lord of lords. Against those who deny His pre-existence and His post-existence, there is a great need to teach that Jesus is the eternal Son of God become man without ceasing to be God. Thereby such heresies as adoptionism, Nestorianism, and docetism will be avoided and no gap between the Jesus of history and the Christ of faith will be forged.

In the presence of differing cosmologies and theories of creation, the third challenge is to be wholly faithful to the biblical doctrine of creation *ex nihilo*. This means that while God sustains and upholds the cosmos He is not part of it and it is not part of Him. With this high view of the created order goes the teaching that man is made in the image and after the likeness of God to enjoy and please Him, that man's relation to God has been broken by the disease of sin, and that man needs redemption.

In the cacophony of voices claiming to proclaim good news in modern society, the fourth challenge is to have a clear view of what is the Gospel of God the Father concerning Jesus Christ, His Son, and to have an overwhelming desire to proclaim it in the power of the Holy Spirit. This clear view of the Gospel is obviously related to sound knowledge of the content of the three doctrines outlined above.

Finally, in the reality of the supermarket of religions and theologies in modern America, and with it the apparent need to major on minors in order to be distinctive in that market, the challenge is to stay joyfully with the proven orthodoxy—i.e., the Trinitarian and Christological doctrine of the content of the Nicene and Athanasian Creeds—and thus major on majors!

In order to face and meet these (and other) challenges, evangelical theologians will need to cultivate a spirituality and piety that flows from genuinely corporate worship, which is truly addressed to the Father, through the Son, in the Spirit. Theology originating and pursued in this atmosphere will be able to avoid the excesses of individualism and idiosyncrasy. We learn from the experience of the Church in history that genuine theology usually arises in meditation upon God's Word and contemplation of His glory.

They will also need to be deeply learned in the Scriptures, in the whole Scriptures and their unity, in the way they were read and interpreted, used in worship and for theology by the Fathers in the early centuries and by the Reformers in the sixteenth century.

Then they will also need to know their own culture and society and how much they are formed by it. Western civilization has gone through many religious, cultural, social, and political changes since the emergence of Protestantism, and so theologians need to be aware of the relation of their own received denominational distinctives to these changes and the movements behind them.

Finally, to come anywhere near meeting the challenges posed by the present situation in Christendom and in western society, evangelical theologians will need to cooperate more closely, to break down barriers caused by working in different disciplines, to engage in dialogue, prayer, and worship together, and to seek to offer what they do as a sacrifice of praise to the Father, through the Son, and in the Spirit.

Works Cited

Altizer, Thomas and William Hamilton. 1966. *Radical Theology and the Death of God*. Indianapolis: Bobbs-Merrill.

Altizer, Thomas. 1966. *Gospel of Christian Atheism*. Philadelphia: Westminster.

Aquinas, Thomas. 1912-36. *Summa Theologiae*. 22 vols. London & New York: Dominican Fathers.

Auerbach, Erich. 1953. *Mimesis: The Representation of Reality in Western Literature*. Translated by W. R. Trask. Princeton, N.J.: Princeton University Press.

Augustine of Hippo. 1963. *The Trinity*. Translated by Stephen McKenna. Washington, D.C.: Catholic University of America Press.

Baillie, Donald M. 1948. *God Was in Christ: An Essay on Incarnation and Atonement*. New York: Scribner.

Barth, Karl. 1921. *The Epistle to the Romans*. Oxford: Oxford University Press.

_____. 1952. *Rudolf Bultmann—Ein Versuch ihn zu verstehen*. Zollikon-Zurich: Evangelischer Verlag.

_____. 1956-75. *Church Dogmatics*. Edited by G. W. Bromiley and T. F. Torrance. Edinburgh: Clark.

Becker, Ernest. 1973. *The Denial of Death*. New York: Free Press.

Berger, Peter L. 1979. *The Heretical Imperative: Contemporary Possibilities of Religious Affirmation*. Garden City, N.Y.: Doubleday.

_____. 1988. "Different Gospels: The Social Sources of

Apostasy." In *Apostate America: The Triumph of Different Gospels*. Edited by Richard Neuhaus. Grand Rapids, Mich.: Eerdmans.

Berkhof, Hendrikus. 1986. *The Christian Faith: An Introduction to the Study of the Bible*. Translated by Sierd Woudstra. Grand Rapids, Mich.: Eerdmans.

Bloesch, Donald G. 1992. *A Theology of Word and Spirit: Authority and Method in Theology*. Downers Grove, Ill.: InterVarsity Press.

Boff, Leonardo. 1978. *Jesus Christ Liberator: A Critical Christology for Our Times*. Translated by P. Hughes. Maryknoll, N.Y.: Orbis.

Bonhoeffer, Dietrich. 1937. *The Cost of Discipleship*. München: Chr. Kaisser Verlag.

_____. 1939, 1954. *Life Together*. Translated by John W. Doberstein. London: SCM Press.

_____. 1963. *Letters and Papers from Prison*. New York: Macmillan.

Bonino, Jose Miguez. 1975. *Doing Theology in a Revolutionary Situation*. Philadelphia: Fortress.

Book of Homilies. 1890. London: S. P. C. K.

Brown, Robert MacFee. 1983, 1992. *Liberation Theology: An Introductory Guide*. Louisville, Ken.: Westminster/John Knox.

Brunner, Emil. 1943. *The Divine-Human Encounter*. Philadelphia: Westminster.

Bultmann, Rudolf. 1948-55. *Kerygma und Mythos*. Edited by Hans-Werner Bartsch. 5 vols. Hamburg: Evangelescher Verlag.

_____. 1951, 1955. *Theology of the New Testament*. 2 vols. Translated by Kendrick Grobel. New York: Scribner.

_____. 1961. *Kerygma and Myth*. New York: Harper & Row.

Buren, Paul Van. 1963. *The Secular Meaning of the Gospel.* New York: Macmillan.

Calvin, John. 1960. *The Institutes of the Christian Religion.* Edited by John T. McNeill. Translated by Ford Lewis Battles. Philadelphia: Westminster.

Catechism of the Catholic Church. 1994. San Francisco: Ignatius.

Clarke, W. N. 1898. *Outline of Christian Theology.* New York: Scribner.

Cone, James H. 1969. *Black Theology and Black Power.* New York: Seabury.

————. 1970. *A Black Theology of Liberation.* Maryknoll, N.Y.: Orbis.

————. 1975. *God of the Oppressed.* New York: Seabury.

Cox, Harvey. 1965, *The Secular City: Secularization and Urbanization in Theological Perspective.* New York: Macmillan.

Croatto, Severino J. 1981. *Exodus: A Hermeneutics of Freedom.* Translated by S. Attanasio. Maryknoll, N.Y.: Orbis.

Denzinger, Heinrich. 1854. *A Manual of the Church's Doctrinal Decisions.*

Dulles, Avery, S.J. 1985. *Models of Revelation.* Garden City, N.Y.: Image.

————. 1992. *The Craft of Theology: From Symbol to System.* New York: Crossroad.

Edwards, David L. 1963. *The Honest to God Debate.* Philadelphia: Westminster Press.

Erickson, Millard J. 1986. *Christian Theology.* 3 vols in one. Grand Rapids, Mich.: Baker.

Fackre, Gabriel J.. 1984. *The Christian Story.* Rev. ed. Grand Rapids, Mich.: Eerdmans.

Fletcher, Joseph. 1966. *Situation Ethics.* Philadelphia: Westminster.

Frei, Hans W. 1974. *The Eclipse of Biblical Narrative*. New Haven, Conn: Yale University Press.

――. 1992. *Types of Christian Theology*. New Haven, Conn.: Yale University Press.

Fries, Heinrich. 1962-63. *Handbuch theologischer Grundbegriffe* (*Handbook of Theological Terms*). München: Kosel-verlag.

Gamber, Klaus. 1993. *The Reform of the Roman Liturgy: Its Problems and Background.* San Juan Capistrano, Calif.: Ina Voca Press.

Geertz, Clifford. 1973. *The Interpretation of Cultures*. New York: Basic.

Gogarten, Friedrich. 1959. *The Reality of Faith*. Philadelphia: Westminster.

Grenz, Stanley J. and Roger E. Olson. 1992. *Twentieth Century Theology: God and the World in a Transitional Age*. Downers Grove, Ill.: InterVarsity.

Gutierrez, Gustavo. 1973. *Theology of Liberation: History, Politics and Salvation*. Translated and edited by Sister Caridad Inda and John Eagleson. Maryknoll, N. Y.: Orbis.

Hamilton, William. 1961. *The New Essence of Christianity*. New York: Association Press.

――. 1964. "Thursday's Child." In *Theology Today* Vol. XX. No. 4. January 1964, 487-495.

Harnack, Adolf von. 1896-99. *History of Dogma*. London: William & Norgate.

――. 1958. *What is Christianity?* 5th ed. London: Ernest Benn.

Healey, Francis G. 1970. *What Theologians Do*. Grand Rapids, Mich.: Eerdmans.

Heidegger, Martin. 1962. *Being and Time*. Translated by John MacQuarrie and Edward Robinson. London: SCM Press.

Henry, Carl F. H. 1979-83. *God, Revelation and Authority*. 6 vols. Waco, Tex: Word.

_____. 1950. *Fifty Years of Protestant Theology*. Boston: Wilde.

Herder, Johann G. 1968. *Ideen zur Philosophie der Geschichte der Menschheit (Reflections on the Philosophy of the History of Mankind)*. Chicago: University of Chicago Press.

Hill, William J., O.P. 1982. *The Three-Personed God*. Washington, D.C.: Catholic University of America Press.

Hodge, Charles. 1872-73. *Systematic Theology*. 3 vols. New York: Scribner.

Holmer, Paul L. 1978. *The Grammar of Faith*. San Francisco: Harper & Row.

Holmes, Urban T. 1981. *Worship Points the Way*. Edited by Malcolm C. Burson. New York: Seabury.

Hunter, James D. 1983. *American Evangelicalism: Conservative Religion and the Quandary of Modernity*. New Brunswick, N.J.: Rutgers University Press.

Ingham, Michael. 1986. *Rites for a New Age*. Toronto: Anglican Book Center.

John of Damascus. *On the Orthodox Faith*. 1963. In *A Select Library of the Post-Nicene Fathers*. Vol. IX. Grand Rapids, Mich.: Eerdmans.

Jung, Carl G. 1923. *Psychological Types*. Translated by Godwin Baynes. New York: Harcourt, Brace & Co.

Kaufman, Gordon. 1975. *An Essay on Theological Method*. Missoula, Mont.: Scholars Press.

Küng, Hans. 1971. *Infallible? An Inquiry*. Translated by Edward Quin. Garden City, N.Y.: Doubleday.

_____. 1988. *Theology for the Third Millennium*. Translated by Peter Heinegg. New York: Doubleday.

Lewis, C. S. 1955. *Surprised by Joy*. New York: Harcourt, Brace & World.

Lindbeck, George A. 1984. *The Nature of Doctrine: Religion and Theology in a Postliberal Age*. Philadelphia: Westminster.

———. 1989. "Scripture, Consensus and Community." In *Biblical Interpretation in Crisis*. Edited by Richard John Neuhaus. Grand Rapids, Mich.: Eerdmans. Originally given at the Ratzinger Conference on Bible and Church.

Lonergan, Bernard, S.J. 1972. *Method in Theology*. New York: Herder & Herder.

———. 1974. "Theology and Man's Future." In *Second Collection: Papers by Bernard J. F. Lonergan*. Edited by William F. J. Ryan and Bernard J. Tyrrell. London: Darton, Longman & Todd.

———. 1974. "Theology in Its New Context." In *Second Collection: Papers by Bernard J. F. Lonergan*. Edited by William F. J. Ryan and Bernard J. Tyrrell. London: Darton, Longman & Todd.

———. 1976. *The Way to Nicea: The Dialectical Development of Trinitarian Theology*. Translated by Conn O'Donovan. Philadelphia: Westminster.

Machen, J. Gresham. 1923. *Christianity and Liberalism*. New York: Macmillan.

Mackintosh, Hugh Ross. 1937. Citing Mark Pattison. In *Types of Modern Theology*. London: Wisbet & Co.

MacQuarrie, John. 1977. *The Principles of Christian Theology*. 2d. ed. New York: Scribner.

Marshall, Bruce D., ed. 1990. *Theology and Dialogue: Essays in Conversation with George Lindbeck*. South Bend, Ind.: University of Notre Dame Press.

Metz, Johann B. 1969, 1971. *Theology of the World*. Translated by William Glen Doepel. New York: Herder & Herder.

Migliore, Daniel L. 1991. *Faith Seeking Understanding: An Introduction to Christian Theology*. Grand Rapids, Mich.: Eerdmans.

Mill, John Stuart. 1859, 1871. *On Liberty*. People's Edition. London: Longman, Green, Reader, & Dyer.

Moltmann, Jürgen. 1967. *Theology of Hope*. New York: Harper & Row.

———. 1969. "Resurrection as Hope." In *Religion, Revolution and the Future*. Translated by M. Douglass Meeks. New York: Scribner.

———. 1981. *Trinity and the Kingdom: The Doctrine of God*. New York: Harper & Row.

Muck, Otto. 1968. *The Transcendental Method*. New York: Herder & Herder.

Niebuhr, H. Richard. 1937. *Kingdom of God in America*. Chicago: Willett Clark & Co.

———. 1941, 1962. *The Meaning of Revelation*. New York: Macmillan.

———. 1951. *Christ and Culture*. New York: Harper.

Niebuhr, Reinhold. 1937. *An Interpretation of Christian Ethics*. 2d. ed. New York: Harper.

———. 1949. *The Nature and Destiny of Man*. New York: Scribner.

Noll, Mark. 1994. *The Scandal of the Evangelical Mind*. Grand Rapids, Mich.: Eerdmans.

Ogden, Schubert M. 1986. *On Theology*. San Francisco: Harper & Row.

Oman, John. 1917. *Grace and Personality*. Cambridge, Mass.: Cambridge University Press.

Otto, Rudolf. 1923. *The Idea of the Holy*. Oxford: Oxford University Press.

Pannenberg, Wolfhart. 1991. *Systematic Theology*. Translated by G. W. Bromiley. Grand Rapids, Mich.: Eerdmans.

Phillips, D. Z. 1979. *Faith and Philosophical Enquiry*. New York: Schocken Books.

Pieper, Franz A. O. 1917, 1950-57. *Christian Dogmatics*. 4 vols. St. Louis: Concordia.

Pinnock, Clark H. 1990. *Tracking the Maze: Finding Your Way*

Through Modern Theology from an Evangelical Perspective. San Francisco: Harper & Row.

Pittenger, W. Norman. 1971. "Process Thought." In *Process Theology: Basic Writings*. Edited by E. H. Cousins. New York: Newman.

Pixley, Jorge V. 1987. *On Exodus: A Liberation Perspective*. Translated by R. R. Barr. Maryknoll, N.Y.: Orbis.

Rahner, Karl, and Herbert Vorgrimler. 1965. *Theological Dictionary*. Edited by Cornelius Ernst. Translated by Richard Strachan. New York: Herder & Herder.

Rahner, Karl. 1978. *Foundations of Christian Faith: An Introduction to the Idea of Christianity*. Translated by William V. Dyche. New York: Seabury.

Ramsey, Ian T. 1973. *Models for Divine Activity*. London: SCM Press.

Rashdall, Hastings. 1919. *The Idea of Atonement in Christian Theology*. London: Macmillan & Co.

Rauschenbusch, Walter. 1917, 1945. *Theology for the Social Gospel*. New York: Abingdon.

Ritschl, Albrecht. 1870-74, 1966. *The Christian Doctrine of Justification and Reconciliation*. 3 vols. Clifton, N.J.: Reference Book Publishers.

Robinson, John and David L. Edwards. 1963. *The "Honest to God" Debate*. Philadelphia: Westminster.

Robinson, John. 1963. *Honest to God*. Philadelphia: Westminster.

———. 1973. *The Human Face of God*. Philadelphia: Westminster.

Ruether, Rosemary Radford. 1983. *Sexism and God-Talk: Toward a Feminist Theology*. Boston: Beacon.

———. 1985. *Women-Church: Theology and Practice*. San Francisco: Harper & Row.

Ryrie, Charles. 1986. *Basic Theology*. Wheaton, Ill.: Victor Books.

Schillebeeckx, Edward. 1981. *Interim Report on the Books "Jesus" and "Christ."* New York: Crossroad.

Schleiermacher, Friedrich. [1799] 1958. *On Religion: Speeches to Its Cultured Despisers.* Translated by John Oman. New York: Harper.

_____. 1830, 1948. *Christian Faith: Presented in Its Inner Connections According to the Fundamentals of the Evangelical Church.* Translated by H. R. Mackintosh. Edinburgh: Clark.

Schreiter, R. J. and Mary C. Hilkert, eds. 1989. *The Praxis of Christian Experience: An Introduction to the Theology of Edward Schillebeeckx.* San Francisco: Harper & Row.

Schüssler Fiorenza, Elisabeth. 1983 *In Memory of Her: A Feminist Theological Reconstruction of Christian Origins.* New York: Crossroad.

_____. 1984. *Bread Not Stone: The Challenge of Feminist Biblical Interpretation.* Boston: Beacon.

_____. 1984. "Emerging Issues in Feminist Biblical Interpretation." In *Christian Feminism: Visions of a New Humanity.* Edited by Judith Weidman. San Francisco: Harper & Row.

Schüssler Fiorenza, Francis and John P. Galvin. 1991. *Systematic Theology: Roman Catholic Perspectives.* 2 vols. Minneapolis: Augsburg Fortress.

Schüssler Fiorenza, Francis. 1991. "Systematic Theology: Task and Methods." In *Systematic Theology: Roman Catholic Perspectives.* Minneapolis: Augsburg Fortress.

Schweitzer, Albert. 1906, 1911. *The Quest of the Historical Jesus.* 2d. ed. New York: A & C Black.

Shepherd, Massey H., Jr. "The Patristic Heritage of the BCP of 1979." In *The Historical Magazine of the Protestant Episcopal Church.* 53, 1980, 221-234.

Simmons, John K. 1986. "Complementism: Liberal Protestant Potential within a Fully Realized Cultural Environment."

In *Liberal Protestantism: Realities and Possibilities*. Edited by Robert S. Michaelsen and Wade C. Roof. New York: Pilgrim.

Sobrino, Jon. 1978. *Christology at the Crossroads: A Latin American Approach*. Translated by John Drury. Maryknoll, N.Y.: Orbis.

Sweet, Leonard I. 1984. "The 1960s: The Crises of Liberal Christianity and the Public Emergence of Evangelicalism." In *Evangelicalism and Modern America*. Edited by George Marsden. Grand Rapids, Mich.: Eerdmans.

———. 1986. "Can a Mainstream Change Its Course?" In *Liberal Protestantism: Realities and Possibilities*. Edited by Robert S. Michaelsen and Wade C. Roof. New York: Pilgrim.

Teilhard de Chardin, Pierre. 1965. *The Phenomenon of Man*. Rev. ed. New York: Harper & Row.

———. 1968. "My Universe." In *Science and Christ*. New York: Harper & Row.

The Fundamentals: A Testimony to the Truth. 1910-15. Compliments of two Christian laymen. Chicago: Testimony Publishing Company.

Tillich, Paul. 1951, 1959, 1967. *Systematic Theology*. 3 vols. in one. Chicago: University of Chicago Press, 1967.

———. 1955. *Biblical Religion and the Search for Ultimate Reality*. Chicago: University of Chicago Press.

Tocqueville, Alexis de. 1969. *Democracy in America*. Translated by George Lawrence. Edited by J. P. Mayer. New York: Doubleday.

Torrance, Thomas F. 1988. *The Trinitarian Faith: The Evangelical Theology of the Ancient Catholic Church*. Edinburgh: Clark.

———. 1990. *Karl Barth: Biblical and Evangelical Theologian*. Edinburgh: Clark.

Tracy, David and Hans Küng, eds. 1989. *Paradigm Change in Theology*. New York: Crossroad.

Tracy, David. 1975. *Blessed Rage for Order: The New Pluralism in Theology*. New York: Seabury.

———. 1981. *The Analogical Imagination: Christian Theology and the Culture of Pluralism*. New York: Crossroad.

———. 1987. *Plurality and Ambiguity: Hermeneutics, Religion, Hope*. San Francisco: Harper & Row.

Troeltsch, Ernst. 1911, 1931. *Social Teaching of the Christian Churches*. Translated by Olive Wyon. New York: Macmillan.

Wells, David F. 1993. *No Place for Truth: Or Whatever Happened to Evangelical Theology*. Grand Rapids, Mich.: Eerdmans.

———. 1994. *God in the Wasteland. The Reality of Truth in a World of Fading Dreams*. Grand Rapids, Mich.: Eerdmans.

Whitman, Walt. 1855, 1897. *Leaves of Grass*. New York: Doubleday, Page & Co.

Williams, Daniel Day. 1952. *What Present-Day Theologians Are Thinking*. New York: Harper.

Young, Pamela Dickey. 1990. *Feminist Theology: Christian Theology in Search of Method*. Minneapolis: Fortress.

Index of Names